UNTO
HIM
SHALL
WE
RETURN

Aug. 1985

Dearest Pat,

   With love to
you and your
mother — for
a more joyous
"return." Love always,
Joanie

UNTO HIM SHALL WE RETURN

*Selections from the
Bahá'í Writings on the
Reality and Immortality
of the Human Soul*

compiled by
HUSHIDAR MOTLAGH

BAHÁ'Í PUBLISHING TRUST
WILMETTE, ILLINOIS 60091

Bahá'í Publishing Trust, Wilmette, Illinois 60091

Library of Congress Cataloging in Publication Data
Main entry under title:

Unto him shall we return.

    Bibliography: p.
    Includes index.
    1. Bahai Faith—Doctrines—Quotations, maxims,
etc.
2. Future life—Bahai Faith—Quotations, maxims, etc.
I. Motlagh, Hushidar, 1934–
BP370.U57   1985   297'.8923   84-24608
ISBN 0-87743-201-5

Design by John Solarz

To the memory of my parents

Contents

PREFACE / *ix*

SELECTIONS FROM THE WRITINGS OF
    BAHÁ'U'LLÁH / *1*

The True Life of Humanity *3*
The Soul and the Life Beyond *6*
Facets of Spiritual Life *21*

SELECTIONS FROM THE WRITINGS OF THE
    BÁB / *31*

Returning to God *33*
Paradise and the Means of Its Attainment *37*
The Rewards of the Faithful *41*

SELECTIONS FROM THE WRITINGS OF 'ABDU'L-
    BAHÁ / *43*

Proofs of Life after Death *45*
The Soul—The True Reality *53*
The Soul's Progress and Condition in This World and
    the Next *74*
The Relationship between the Living and the Dead *97*
The Imperishable Gift *108*

GEMS FOR MEDITATION / *113*

PRAYERS FOR THE DEPARTED / *119*

REFERENCES / *131*

INDEX / *137*

Preface

Are humans mortal or immortal? Is death a door to doom and extinction or a portal to a new life, abundant and everlasting? Are heaven and hell real? What is the kingdom of heaven like? Is it static or progressive? What does "hell fire" signify? What is the purpose of earthly life? Is earth the place of planting for a heavenly harvest? What virtues must one gain here to be prepared for hereafter? Who will guard infants who die an early death? What is the soul? Can its reality and immortality be confirmed by reason?

These are but a few of the questions people have asked about themselves and their destiny since the dawn of history, questions whose resolution can exert far-reaching influences in our lives.

Who is capable of resolving such mysteries? Who can claim true knowledge of the human soul and its ultimate destiny? Bahá'ís, members of the world's latest independent religion, believe that such knowledge is granted only to great Teachers or Messengers from God Who dawn periodically to bestow new truths measured to an ever-advancing civilization.

God, Bahá'ís believe, has once again spoken to us through another of His great Teachers or Messengers, Bahá'u'lláh, Who has revealed new teachings aimed at enriching our lives both

individually and collectively—teachings that point
to a common and eternal destiny shared by
everyone.

Bahá'u'lláh wrote over a hundred volumes
illuminating and expanding every aspect of human
life. This compilation focuses mainly on His
teachings on the reality and immortality of the
human soul, the purpose of our lives here on this
planet, and the continuation of such a purpose into
the mysterious realms beyond. It contains selections
gleaned from His writings as well as those of His
Forerunner, the Báb, and His Successor and
appointed Interpreter of His teachings,
'Abdu'l-Bahá.

Though the selections contained here have
been published elsewhere, they have been compiled
and arranged in this volume to portray a clearer
vision of the purpose and meaning of our lives—
both here and hereafter. This compilation presents a
measure of knowledge adapted to the maturity of
our age, truths whose revelation is foretold by
all the great Messengers of the past. Its theme is as
ancient as man, its message as fresh as the dawn.

Not only do the teachings of Bahá'u'lláh deal
with life after death, but far more abundantly
with life here on this planet. In the light of His
knowledge, our lives glow with a hope and a
purpose that reach out from the finite to the
infinite; and through the power of His words our
thoughts turn into the threads that bind us to
the ultimate Source and Essence of our being.

As Bahá'u'lláh stirs us by a vision and a hope
for a glorious realm beyond, so does He grant us the
knowledge for building a splendid and lasting

kingdom here on this planet. The realization of
"Thy kingdom come on earth as it is in heaven" is
His foremost mission. He offers workable solutions
to the needs of humankind for at least the next
thousand years. He guides us toward a glorious and
ever-advancing civilization foretold by all the
prophets of the past.

The pillars of the new civilization are the
unified peoples and races of the earth who
are working together in a spirit of love and
fellowship, inspired by their allegiance to one
universal faith. To achieve the goal of unity
Bahá'u'lláh introduced many teachings, among
them the following:

- Truth is one, but traditions are many. No
one should follow blindly the path of his ancestors
but should, instead, seek the truth for himself.

- All religions come from the same Source.
They all express aspects of the same Truth, and they
all reflect the divine wisdom revealed progressively
according to the needs and maturity of humankind.

- Religion is the cause of unity, harmony,
and peace. If it becomes an instrument of division
or prejudice, it is best avoided.

- Religion and science are perfect partners.
Their powers, their workings, and their influence
must be brought into absolute harmony.

- Sex descrimination must be abolished.

- Prejudice must be uprooted.

- Universal peace must be established.

- Universal and compulsory education must
be provided for all.

- Extremes of wealth and poverty must be
eliminated both through laws and through the

recognition of the individual's spiritual
responsibility.

■ A universal language must be adopted and
taught throughout the world.

■ A world government must reign, regulating
all international relations.

When Bahá'u'lláh proclaimed these teachings
in the second half of the nineteenth century,
humankind as a whole was not mature enough to
recognize their urgent necessity. As time goes
on, the world moves gradually toward their
realization. Let us hope that humankind will
respond to Bahá'u'lláh's call for unity and peace in
due time, before the prevailing world order has
collapsed under the overwhelming weight of war,
poverty, prejudice, and spiritual hunger.

"O friends! It behooveth you to refresh and
revive your souls through the gracious favors which
in this Divine, this soul-stirring Springtime are
being showered upon you. The Daystar of His great
glory hath shed its radiance upon you, and the
clouds of His limitless grace have overshadowed
you. How high the reward of him that hath
not deprived himself of so great a bounty, nor failed
to recognize the beauty of his Best-Beloved in
this, His new attire."

"Wert thou to attain to but a dewdrop of the
crystal waters of divine knowledge, thou wouldst
readily realize that true life is not the life of the
flesh but the life of the spirit. For the life of
the flesh is common to both men and animals,
whereas the life of the spirit is possessed only by the

pure in heart who have quaffed from the ocean of
faith and partaken of the fruit of certitude. This life
knoweth no death, and this existence is crowned
by immortality. Even as it hath been said: "He who
is a true believer liveth both in this world and in the
world to come."

Then [at death] he will be united with me. Be certain of that.

BHAGAVAD-GITA 8:4

Then shall the dust return to the earth as it was: and the spirit shall return unto God who gave it.

ECCLESIASTES 12:7

Soon ye return to us: and we will let you know what ye have done!

For unto God shall be the final gathering.

QUR'ÁN 10:24; 35:19

All men have proceeded from God and unto Him shall all return.

THE BÁB

Verily, we are God's. . . . And unto Him we do return.

BAHÁ'U'LLÁH

*Selections from the
Writings of Bahá'u'lláh*

The True Life of Humanity

The Joy Destined for Humanity in the Life Beyond

SORROW not if, in these days and on this earthly
plane, things contrary to your wishes have been
ordained and manifested by God, for days of
blissful joy, of heavenly delight, are assuredly in
store for you. Worlds, holy and spiritually glorious,
will be unveiled to your eyes. You are destined by
Him, in this world and hereafter, to partake of their
benefits, to share in their joys, and to obtain a
portion of their sustaining grace. To each and every
one of them you will, no doubt, attain.   1

The True Life of the Spirit

WERT thou to attain to but a dewdrop of the
crystal waters of divine knowledge, thou
wouldst readily realize that true life is not the life of
the flesh but the life of the spirit. For the life of the
flesh is common to both men and animals,
whereas the life of the spirit is possessed only by the
pure in heart who have quaffed from the ocean of
faith and partaken of the fruit of certitude. This life
knoweth no death, and this existence is crowned
by immortality. Even as it hath been said: "He who
is a true believer liveth both in this world and in the
world to come." If by "life" be meant this earthly
life, it is evident that death must needs overtake it. 2

Unique Capacities Conferred on Humankind

HAVING created the world and all that liveth and moveth therein, He,* through the direct operation of His unconstrained and sovereign Will, chose to confer upon man the unique distinction and capacity to know Him and to love Him—a capacity that must needs be regarded as the generating impulse and the primary purpose underlying the whole of creation. . . . Upon the inmost reality of each and every created thing He hath shed the light of one of His names, and made it a recipient of the glory of one of His attributes. Upon the reality of man, however, He hath focused the radiance of all of His names and attributes, and made it a mirror of His own Self. Alone of all created things man hath been singled out for so great a favor, so enduring a bounty.   3

ALL praise and glory be to God Who, through the power of His might, hath delivered His creation from the nakedness of nonexistence, and clothed it with the mantle of life. From among all created things He hath singled out for His special favor the pure, the gem-like reality of man, and invested it with a unique capacity of knowing Him and of reflecting the greatness of His glory. This twofold distinction conferred upon him hath cleansed away from his heart the rust of every vain desire, and made him worthy of the vesture

---

*God.

with which his Creator hath deigned to clothe him. It hath served to rescue his soul from the wretchedness of ignorance.

This robe with which the body and soul of man hath been adorned is the very foundation of his well-being and development. Oh, how blessed the day when, aided by the grace and might of the one true God, man will have freed himself from the bondage and corruption of the world and all that is therein, and will have attained unto true and abiding rest beneath the shadow of the Tree of Knowledge!   4

The Challenge of Manifesting Potential

AND now, concerning thy question regarding the creation of man. Know thou that all men have been created in the nature made by God, the Guardian, the Self-Subsisting. Unto each one hath been prescribed a preordained measure, as decreed in God's mighty and guarded Tablets. All that which ye potentially possess can, however, be manifested only as a result of your own volition. Your own acts testify to this truth.   5

The Soul and the Life Beyond

The Nature of the Soul

Thou hast asked Me concerning the nature of the soul. Know, verily, that the soul is a sign of God, a heavenly gem whose reality the most learned of men hath failed to grasp, and whose mystery no mind, however acute, can ever hope to unravel. It is the first among all created things to declare the excellence of its Creator, the first to recognize His glory, to cleave to His truth, and to bow down in adoration before Him. If it be faithful to God, it will reflect His light, and will, eventually, return unto Him. If it fail, however, in its allegiance to its Creator, it will become a victim to self and passion, and will, in the end, sink in their depths.

Whoso hath, in this Day, refused to allow the doubts and fancies of men to turn him away from Him Who is the Eternal Truth, and hath not suffered the tumult provoked by the ecclesiastical and secular authorities to deter him from recognizing His Message, such a man will be regarded by God, the Lord of all men, as one of His mighty signs, and will be numbered among them whose names have been inscribed by the Pen of the Most High in His Book. Blessed is he that hath recognized the true stature of such a soul, that hath acknowledged its station, and discovered its virtues.

Much hath been written in the books of old

concerning the various stages in the development of the soul, such as concupiscence, irascibility, inspiration, benevolence, contentment, divine good-pleasure, and the like; the Pen of the Most High, however, is disinclined to dwell upon them. Every soul that walketh humbly with its God, in this Day, and cleaveth unto Him, shall find itself invested with the honor and glory of all goodly names and stations.

When man is asleep, his soul can, in no wise, be said to have been inherently affected by any external object. It is not susceptible of any change in its original state or character. Any variation in its functions is to be ascribed to external causes. It is to these external influences that any variations in its environment, its understanding, and perception should be attributed.

Consider the human eye. Though it hath the faculty of perceiving all created things, yet the slightest impediment may so obstruct its vision as to deprive it of the power of discerning any object whatsoever. Magnified be the name of Him Who hath created, and is the Cause of, these causes, Who hath ordained that every change and variation in the world of being be made dependent upon them. Every created thing in the whole universe is but a door leading into His knowledge, a sign of His sovereignty, a revelation of His names, a symbol of His majesty, a token of His power, a means of admittance into His straight Path. . . .

Verily I say, the human soul is, in its essence, one of the signs of God, a mystery among His mysteries. It is one of the mighty signs of the Almighty, the harbinger that proclaimeth the reality of all the worlds of God. Within it lieth concealed that which the world is now utterly incapable of apprehending. Ponder in thine heart the revelation of the Soul of God that pervadeth all His Laws, and contrast it with that base and appetitive nature that hath rebelled against Him, that forbiddeth men to turn unto the Lord of Names, and impelleth them to walk after their lusts and wickedness. Such a soul hath, in truth, wandered far in the path of error. . . .

Thou hast, moreover, asked Me concerning the state of the soul after its separation from the body. Know thou, of a truth, that if the soul of man hath walked in the ways of God, it will, assuredly, return and be gathered to the glory of the Beloved. By the righteousness of God! It shall attain a station such as no pen can depict, or tongue describe. The soul that hath remained faithful to the Cause of God, and stood unwaveringly firm in His Path, shall, after his ascension, be possessed of such power that all the worlds which the Almighty hath created can benefit through him. Such a soul provideth, at the bidding of the Ideal King and Divine Educator, the pure leaven that leaveneth the world of being, and furnisheth the power through which the arts and wonders of the world are made manifest. Consider how meal needeth leaven to be leavened with. Those souls that are the symbols of detachment are the leaven of the world. Meditate on this, and be of the thankful.

In several of Our Tablets We have referred to this theme, and have set forth the various stages in the development of the soul. Verily I say, the human soul is exalted above all egress and

regress. It is still, and yet it soareth; it moveth, and
yet it is still. It is, in itself, a testimony that
beareth witness to the existence of a world that is
contingent, as well as to the reality of a world that
hath neither beginning nor end. Behold how the
dream thou hast dreamed is, after the lapse of many
years, reenacted before thine eyes. Consider how
strange is the mystery of the world that appeareth
to thee in thy dream. Ponder in thine heart upon
the unsearchable wisdom of God, and meditate on
its manifold revelations. . . .   6

The State of the Soul after Death

AND now concerning thy question regarding the
soul of man and its survival after death.
Know thou of a truth that the soul, after its
separation from the body, will continue to progress
until it attaineth the presence of God, in a state
and condition which neither the revolution of ages
and centuries, nor the changes and chances of
this world, can alter. It will endure as long as the
Kingdom of God, His sovereignty, His dominion
and power will endure. It will manifest the signs of
God and His attributes, and will reveal His
loving-kindness and bounty. The movement of My
Pen is stilled when it attempteth to befittingly
describe the loftiness and glory of so exalted
a station. The honor with which the Hand of
Mercy will invest the soul is such as no tongue can
adequately reveal, nor any other earthly agency
describe. Blessed is the soul which, at the hour of
its separation from the body, is sanctified from

the vain imaginings of the peoples of the world.
Such a soul liveth and moveth in accordance with
the Will of its Creator, and entereth the all-highest
Paradise. The Maids of Heaven, inmates of the
loftiest mansions, will circle around it, and
the Prophets of God and His chosen ones will seek
its companionship. With them that soul will
freely converse, and will recount unto them that
which it hath been made to endure in the path of
God, the Lord of all worlds. If any man be told that
which hath been ordained for such a soul in the
worlds of God, the Lord of the throne on high and
of earth below, his whole being will instantly
blaze out in his great longing to attain that most
exalted, that sanctified and resplendent station. . . .
The nature of the soul after death can never be
described, nor is it meet and permissible to reveal its
whole character to the eyes of men. The Prophets
and Messengers of God have been sent down for the
sole purpose of guiding mankind to the straight
Path of Truth. The purpose underlying their
revelation hath been to educate all men, that they
may, at the hour of death, ascend, in the utmost
purity and sanctity and with absolute detachment,
to the throne of the Most High. The light
which these souls radiate is responsible for the
progress of the world and the advancement of its
peoples. They are like unto leaven which leaveneth
the world of being, and constitute the animating
force through which the arts and wonders of
the world are made manifest. Through them the
clouds rain their bounty upon men, and the
earth bringeth forth its fruits. All things must needs
have a cause, a motive power, an animating

principle. These souls and symbols of detachment
have provided, and will continue to provide, the
supreme moving impulse in the world of being. The
world beyond is as different from this world as this
world is different from that of the child while
still in the womb of its mother. When the soul
attaineth the Presence of God, it will assume the
form that best befitteth its immortality and is
worthy of its celestial habitation. Such an existence
is a contingent and not an absolute existence,
inasmuch as the former is preceded by a cause,
whilst the latter is independent thereof. Absolute
existence is strictly confined to God, exalted be His
glory. Well is it with them that apprehend this
truth. Wert thou to ponder in thine heart the
behavior of the Prophets of God, thou wouldst
assuredly and readily testify that there must needs
be other worlds besides this world. The majority of
the truly wise and learned have, throughout the
ages, as it hath been recorded by the Pen of Glory
in the Tablet of Wisdom, borne witness to the truth
of that which the holy Writ of God hath revealed.
Even the materialists have testified in their writings
to the wisdom of these divinely appointed
Messengers, and have regarded the references made
by the Prophets to Paradise, to hell fire, to future
reward and punishment, to have been actuated by a
desire to educate and uplift the souls of men.
Consider, therefore, how the generality of mankind,
whatever their beliefs or theories, have recognized
the excellence, and admitted the superiority, of
these Prophets of God. These Gems of Detachment
are acclaimed by some as the embodiments of
wisdom, while others believe them to be the

mouthpiece of God Himself. How could such Souls
have consented to surrender themselves unto their
enemies if they believed all the worlds of God to
have been reduced to this earthly life? Would they
have willingly suffered such afflictions and torments
as no man hath ever experienced or witnessed?

7

The Continuation of Consciousness

AND now concerning thy question whether
human souls continue to be conscious one of
another after their separation from the body. Know
thou that the souls of the people of Bahá, who
have entered and been established within the
Crimson Ark, shall associate and commune
intimately one with another, and shall be so closely
associated in their lives, their aspirations, their
aims and strivings as to be even as one soul. They
are indeed the ones who are well-informed, who are
keen-sighted, and who are endued with
understanding. Thus hath it been decreed by Him
Who is the All-Knowing, the All-Wise.

The people of Bahá, who are the inmates of
the Ark of God, are, one and all, well aware of one
another's state and condition, and are united in
the bonds of intimacy and fellowship. Such a state,
however, must depend upon their faith and their
conduct. They that are of the same grade and
station are fully aware of one another's capacity,
character, accomplishments and merits. They that
are of a lower grade, however, are incapable of
comprehending adequately the station, or of
estimating the merits, of those that rank above
them. Each shall receive his share from thy Lord.

Blessed is the man that hath turned his face towards God, and walked steadfastly in His love, until his soul hath winged its flight unto God, the Sovereign Lord of all, the Most Powerful, the Ever-Forgiving, the All-Merciful.

The souls of the infidels, however, shall—and to this I bear witness—when breathing their last be made aware of the good things that have escaped them, and shall bemoan their plight, and shall humble themselves before God. They shall continue doing so after the separation of their souls from their bodies.

It is clear and evident that all men shall, after their physical death, estimate the worth of their deeds, and realize all that their hands have wrought. I swear by the Daystar that shineth above the horizon of divine power! They that are the followers of the one true God shall, the moment they depart out of this life, experience such joy and gladness as would be impossible to describe, while they that live in error shall be seized with such fear and trembling, and shall be filled with such consternation, as nothing can exceed. Well is it with him that hath quaffed the choice and incorruptible wine of faith through the gracious favor and the manifold bounties of Him Who is the Lord of all Faiths. . . .   8

The Independence of the Soul from Physical Limitations

THOU hast asked Me whether man, as apart from the Prophets of God and His chosen ones, will retain, after his physical death, the selfsame individuality, personality, consciousness, and understanding that characterize his life in this world. If this should be the case, how is it, thou hast observed, that whereas such slight injuries to his mental faculties as fainting and severe illness deprive him of his understanding and consciousness, his death, which must involve the decomposition of his body and the dissolution of its elements, is powerless to destroy that understanding and extinguish that consciousness? How can anyone imagine that man's consciousness and personality will be maintained, when the very instruments necessary to their existence and function will have completely disintegrated?

Know thou that the soul of man is exalted above and is independent of all infirmities of body or mind. That a sick person showeth signs of weakness is due to the hindrances that interpose themselves between his soul and his body, for the soul itself remaineth unaffected by any bodily ailments. Consider the light of the lamp. Though an external object may interfere with its radiance, the light itself continueth to shine with undiminished power. In like manner, every malady afflicting the body of man is an impediment that preventeth the soul from manifesting its inherent might and power. When it leaveth the body, however, it will evince such ascendancy, and reveal such influence as no force on earth can equal. Every pure, every refined and sanctified soul will be endowed with tremendous power, and shall rejoice with exceeding gladness.

Consider the lamp which is hidden under a

bushel. Though its light be shining, yet its radiance
is concealed from men. Likewise, consider the sun
which hath been obscured by the clouds. Observe
how its splendor appeareth to have diminished,
when in reality the source of that light hath
remained unchanged. The soul of man should be
likened unto this sun, and all things on earth should
be regarded as his body. So long as no external
impediment interveneth between them, the body
will, in its entirety, continue to reflect the light of
the soul, and to be sustained by its power. As
soon as, however, a veil interposeth itself between
them, the brightness of that light seemeth to lessen.

Consider again the sun when it is completely
hidden behind the clouds. Though the earth is
still illumined with its light, yet the measure of
light which it receiveth is considerably reduced.
Not until the clouds have dispersed can the sun
shine again in the plenitude of its glory. Neither the
presence of the cloud nor its absence can, in any
way, affect the inherent splendor of the sun.
The soul of man is the sun by which his body is
illumined, and from which it draweth its
sustenance, and should be so regarded.   9

The Countless Worlds of God

As to thy question concerning the worlds of God.
Know thou of a truth that the worlds of God
are countless in their number, and infinite in
their range. None can reckon or comprehend them
except God, the All-Knowing, the All-Wise.

Consider thy state when asleep. Verily, I say, this phenomenon is the most mysterious of the signs of God amongst men, were they to ponder it in their hearts. Behold how the thing which thou hast seen in thy dream is, after a considerable lapse of time, fully realized. Had the world in which thou didst find thyself in thy dream been identical with the world in which thou livest, it would have been necessary for the event occurring in that dream to have transpired in this world at the very moment of its occurrence. Were it so, you yourself would have borne witness unto it. This being not the case, however, it must necessarily follow that the world in which thou livest is different and apart from that which thou hast experienced in thy dream. This latter world hath neither beginning nor end. It would be true if thou wert to contend that this same world is, as decreed by the All-Glorious and Almighty God, within thy proper self and is wrapped up within thee. It would equally be true to maintain that thy spirit, having transcended the limitations of sleep and having stripped itself of all earthly attachment, hath, by the act of God, been made to traverse a realm which lieth hidden in the innermost reality of this world. Verily I say, the creation of God embraceth worlds besides this world, and creatures apart from these creatures. In each of these worlds He hath ordained things which none can search except Himself, the All-Searching, the All-Wise. Do thou meditate on that which We have revealed unto thee, that thou mayest discover the purpose of God, thy Lord, and the Lord of all worlds. In these

words the mysteries of divine wisdom have been
treasured.   **10**

Dreams As Evidence of a Life Beyond

ONE of the created phenomena is the dream.
Behold how many secrets are deposited
therein, how many wisdoms treasured up, how
many worlds concealed. Observe, how thou
art asleep in a dwelling, and its doors are barred; on
a sudden thou findest thyself in a far-off city,
which thou enterest without moving thy feet or
wearying thy body; without using thine eyes, thou
seest; without taxing thine ears, thou hearest;
without a tongue, thou speakest. And perchance
when ten years are gone, thou wilt witness in the
outer world the very things thou hast dreamed
tonight.

Now there are many wisdoms to ponder in the
dream. . . . First, what is this world, where
without eye and ear and hand and tongue a man
puts all of these to use? Second, how is it that in the
outer world thou seest today the effect of a dream,
when thou didst vision it in the world of sleep some
ten years past? Consider the difference between
these two worlds and the mysteries which
they conceal, that thou mayest attain to divine
confirmations and heavenly discoveries and enter
the regions of holiness.

God, the Exalted, hath placed these signs in
men, to the end that philosophers may not deny the
mysteries of the life beyond nor belittle that which
hath been promised them.   **11**

The Rational Faculty

Consider the rational faculty* with which God hath endowed the essence of man. Examine thine own self, and behold how thy motion and stillness, thy will and purpose, thy sight and hearing, thy sense of smell and power of speech, and whatever else is related to, or transcendeth, thy physical senses or spiritual perceptions, all proceed from, and owe their existence to, this same faculty. So closely are they related unto it that, if in less than the twinkling of an eye its relationship to the human body be severed, each and every one of these senses will cease immediately to exercise its function, and will be deprived of the power to manifest the evidences of its activity. It is indubitably clear and evident that each of these aforementioned instruments has depended, and will ever continue to depend, for its proper functioning on this rational faculty, which should be regarded as a sign of the revelation of Him Who is the sovereign Lord of all. Through its manifestation all these names and attributes have been revealed, and by the suspension of its action they are all destroyed and perish.

It would be wholly untrue to maintain that this faculty is the same as the power of vision, inasmuch as the power of vision is derived from it and acteth in dependence upon it. It would, likewise, be idle to contend that this faculty can be identified with the sense of hearing, as the sense

---

*See footnote on p. 60.

of hearing receiveth from the rational faculty the
requisite energy for performing its functions.

This same relationship bindeth this faculty
with whatsoever hath been the recipient of
these names and attributes within the human
temple. These diverse names and revealed attributes
have been generated through the agency of this
sign of God. Immeasurably exalted is this sign, in
its essence and reality, above all such names and
attributes. Nay, all else besides it will, when
compared with its glory, fade into utter nothingness
and become a thing forgotten.

Wert thou to ponder in thine heart, from now
until the end that hath no end, and with all the
concentrated intelligence and understanding which
the greatest minds have attained in the past or will
attain in the future, this divinely ordained and
subtle Reality, this sign of the revelation of the All-
Abiding, All-Glorious God, thou wilt fail to
comprehend its mystery or to appraise its virtue.

12

Death, Fate, and Predestination

O THOU who art the fruit of My Tree and the
leaf thereof! On thee be My glory and
My mercy. Let not thine heart grieve over what
hath befallen thee. Wert thou to scan the pages of
the Book of Life, thou wouldst, most certainly,
discover that which would dissipate thy sorrows and
dissolve thine anguish.

Know thou, O fruit of My Tree, that the
decrees of the Sovereign Ordainer, as related to fate
and predestination, are of two kinds. Both are to

be obeyed and accepted. The one is irrevocable, the other is, as termed by men, impending. To the former all must unreservedly submit, inasmuch as it is fixed and settled. God, however, is able to alter or repeal it. As the harm that must result from such a change will be greater than if the decree had remained unaltered, all, therefore, should willingly acquiesce in what God hath willed and confidently abide by the same.

The decree that is impending, however, is such that prayer and entreaty can succeed in averting it.

God grant that thou who art the fruit of My Tree, and they that are associated with thee, may be shielded from its evil consequences.

Say: O God, my God! Thou has committed into mine hands a trust from Thee, and hast now according to the good-pleasure of Thy Will called it back to Thyself. It is not for me, who am a handmaid of Thine, to say, whence is this to me or wherefore hath it happened, inasmuch as Thou art glorified in all Thine acts, and art to be obeyed in Thy decree.   **13**

Facets of the Spiritual Life

The High Destiny of the True Believer

IT is clear and evident that when the veils that conceal the realities of the manifestations of the Names and Attributes of God, nay of all created things visible or invisible, have been rent asunder, nothing except the Sign of God will remain—a sign which He, Himself, hath placed within these realities. This sign will endure as long as is the wish of the Lord thy God, the Lord of the heavens and of the earth. If such be the blessings conferred on all created things, how superior must be the destiny of the true believer, whose existence and life are to be regarded as the originating purpose of all creation. Just as the conception of faith hath existed from the beginning that hath no beginning, and will endure till the end that hath no end, in like manner will the true believer eternally live and endure. His spirit will everlastingly circle round the Will of God. He will last as long as God, Himself, will last. He is revealed through the Revelation of God, and is hidden at His bidding. It is evident that the loftiest mansions in the Realm of Immortality have been ordained as the habitation of them that have truly believed in God and in His signs. Death can never invade that holy seat. Thus have We entrusted thee with the signs of Thy Lord, that thou mayest persevere in thy love for Him, and be of them that comprehend this truth. 14

21

The Attainment of Paradise

As to Paradise: It is a reality and there can be no doubt about it, and now in this world it is realized through love of Me and My good-pleasure. Whosoever attaineth unto it God will aid him in this world below, and after death He will enable him to gain admittance into Paradise whose vastness is as that of heaven and earth. Therein the Maids of glory and holiness will wait upon him in the daytime and in the night season, while the daystar of the unfading beauty of his Lord will at all times shed its radiance upon him, and he will shine so brightly that no one shall bear to gaze at him. Such is the dispensation of Providence, yet the people are shut out by a grievous veil. Likewise apprehend thou the nature of hell fire, and be of them that truly believe. For every act performed there shall be a recompense according to the estimate of God, and unto this the very ordinances and prohibitions prescribed by the Almighty amply bear witness. For surely if deeds were not rewarded and yielded no fruit, then the Cause of God—exalted is He—would prove futile. Immeasurably high is He exalted above such blasphemies! However, unto them that are rid of all attachments a deed is, verily, its own reward.   **15**

The Meaning of Spiritual Rebirth

Even as Jesus said: "Ye must be born again." Again He saith: "Except a man be born of water and of the Spirit, he cannot enter into the

Kingdom of God. That which is born of the flesh is
flesh; and that which is born of the Spirit is
spirit."* The purport of these words is that
whosoever in every dispensation is born of the
Spirit and is quickened by the breath of the
Manifestation of Holiness, he verily is of those that
have attained unto "life" and "resurrection" and
have entered into the "paradise" of the love of God.
And whosoever is not of them is condemned to
"death" and "deprivation," to the "fire" of unbelief,
and to the "wrath" of God. In all the scriptures,
the books and chronicles, the sentence of death, of
fire, of blindness, of want of understanding and
hearing, hath been pronounced against those whose
lips have tasted not the ethereal cup of true
knowledge, and whose hearts have been deprived of
the grace of the holy Spirit in their day.   16

Remoteness from God

WHOSO hath failed to recognize Him† will
have condemned himself to the misery of
remoteness, a remoteness which is naught but utter
nothingness and the essence of the nethermost
fire. Such will be his fate, though to outward
seeming he may occupy the earth's loftiest seats and
be established upon its most exalted throne.   17

---

*John 3:7, 5–6.
†God.

The Vanity of the World

THE world is but a show, vain and empty, a mere nothing, bearing the semblance of reality. Set not your affections upon it. Break not the bond that uniteth you with your Creator, and be not of those that have erred and strayed from His ways. Verily I say, the world is like the vapor in a desert, which the thirsty dreameth to be water and striveth after it with all his might, until when he cometh unto it, he findeth it to be mere illusion.   **18**

A Haven against the Changes of This Life

THE generations that have gone on before you— whither are they fled? And those round whom in life circled the fairest and the loveliest of the land, where now are they? Profit by their example, O people, and be not of them that are gone astray.

Others erelong will lay hands on what ye possess, and enter into your habitations. Incline your ears to My words, and be not numbered among the foolish.

For every one of you his paramount duty is to choose for himself that on which no other may infringe and none usurp from him. Such a thing— and to this the Almighty is My witness—is the love of God, could ye but perceive it.

Build ye for yourselves such houses as the rain and floods can never destroy, which shall protect you from the changes and chances of this life. This is the instruction of Him Whom the world hath wronged and forsaken.   **19**

The Evanescence of Earth's Treasures

Exultest thou over the treasures thou dost possess, knowing they shall perish? Rejoicest thou in that thou rulest a span of earth, when the whole world, in the estimation of the people of Bahá, is worth as much as the black in the eye of a dead ant? Abandon it unto such as have set their affections upon it, and turn thou unto Him Who is the Desire of the world. Whither are gone the proud and their palaces? Gaze thou into their tombs, that thou mayest profit by this example, inasmuch as We made it a lesson unto every beholder. Were the breezes of Revelation to seize thee, thou wouldst flee the world, and turn unto the Kingdom, and wouldst expend all thou possessest, that thou mayest draw nigh unto this sublime Vision.   20

The Swiftness of Passing Days

Night hath succeeded day, and day hath succeeded night, and the hours and moments of your lives have come and gone, and yet none of you hath, for one instant, consented to detach himself from that which perisheth. Bestir yourselves, that the brief moments that are still yours may not be dissipated and lost. Even as the swiftness of lightning your days shall pass, and your bodies shall be laid to rest beneath a canopy of dust. What can ye then achieve? How can ye atone for your past failure?

The everlasting Candle shineth in its naked

glory. Behold how it hath consumed every mortal
veil. O ye moth-like lovers of His light! Brave every
danger, and consecrate your souls to its consuming
flame. O ye that thirst after Him! Strip yourselves
of every earthly affection, and hasten to embrace
your Beloved. With a zest that none can equal make
haste to attain unto Him. The Flower, thus far
hidden from the sight of men, is unveiled to your
eyes. In the open radiance of His glory He standeth
before you. His voice summoneth all the holy and
sanctified beings to come and be united with
Him. Happy is he that turneth thereunto; well is it
with him that hath attained, and gazed on the
light of so wondrous a countenance.   21

The Transience of Earthly Life

BEWARE lest the transitory things of human life
withhold you from turning unto God, the True
One. Ponder ye in your hearts the world and its
conflicts and changes, so that ye may discern
its merit and the station of those who have set their
hearts upon it and have turned away from that
which hath been sent down in Our Preserved
Tablet.   22

The Summons to Weigh Every Action

SET before thine eyes God's unerring Balance and,
as one standing in His Presence, weigh in that
Balance thine actions every day, every moment
of thy life. Bring thyself to account ere thou art

summoned to a reckoning, on the Day when
no man shall have strength to stand for fear of God,
the Day when the hearts of the heedless ones shall
be made to tremble.   **23**

The Day of Accounting

Ye will most certainly be called upon to answer
for His trust on the day when the Balance
of Justice shall be set, the day when unto everyone
shall be rendered his due, when the doings of all
men, be they rich or poor, shall be weighed.   **24**

Ye, and all ye possess, shall pass away. Ye shall,
most certainly, return to God, and shall be
called to account for your doings in the presence of
Him Who shall gather together the entire
creation. . . .   **25**

Blessings for the Pure and Holy

We verily behold your actions. If We perceive
from them the sweet-smelling savor of
purity and holiness, We will most certainly bless
you. Then will the tongues of the inmates of
Paradise utter your praise and magnify your names
amidst them who have drawn nigh unto God.   **26**

The Injunction to Walk in the Ways of God

Walk ye, during the few remaining days of
your life, in the ways of the one true God.
Your days shall pass away as have the days of

them who were before you. To dust shall ye return, even as your fathers of old did return.   **27**

The Station of Believers

As to those that have tasted of the fruit of man's earthly existence, which is the recognition of the one true God, exalted be His glory, their life hereafter is such as We are unable to describe. The knowledge thereof is with God, alone, the Lord of all worlds.   **28**

The Eternal Recognition of the Lovers of God

SAY: I swear by the righteousness of God! Erelong the pomp of the ministers of state and the ascendancy of the rulers shall pass away, the palaces of the potentates shall be laid waste and the imposing buildings of the emperors reduced to dust, but what shall endure is that which We have ordained for you in the Kingdom. It behooveth you, O people, to make the utmost endeavor that your names may be mentioned before the Throne and ye may bring forth that which will immortalize your memories throughout the eternity of God, the Lord of all being.   **29**

The Blessedness of Days Devoted to God

SAY: Rejoice not in the things ye possess; tonight they are yours, tomorrow others will possess them. Thus warneth you He Who is the All-

Knowing, the All-Informed. Say: Can ye claim that what ye own is lasting or secure? Nay! By Myself, the All-Merciful. The days of your life flee away as a breath of wind, and all your pomp and glory shall be folded up as were the pomp and glory of those gone before you. Reflect, O people! What hath become of your bygone days, your lost centuries? Happy the days that have been consecrated to the remembrance of God, and blessed the hours which have been spent in praise of Him Who is the All-Wise. By My life! Neither the pomp of the mighty, nor the wealth of the rich, nor even the ascendancy of the ungodly will endure. All will perish, at a word from Him. He, verily, is the All-Powerful, the All-Compelling, the Almighty. What advantage is there in the earthly things which men possess? That which shall profit them, they have utterly neglected. Erelong, they will awake from their slumber, and find themselves unable to obtain that which hath escaped them in the days of their Lord, the Almighty, the All-Praised. Did they but know it, they would renounce their all, that their names may be mentioned before His throne. They, verily, are accounted among the dead.   30

Surrender to the Beloved

HEAR Me, ye mortal birds! In the Rose Garden of changeless splendor a Flower hath begun to bloom, compared to which every other flower is but a thorn, and before the brightness of Whose glory the very essence of beauty must pale and wither. Arise, therefore, and, with the whole enthusiasm of your hearts, with all the eagerness of your souls, the full fervor of your will, and the concentrated efforts of your entire being, strive to attain the paradise of His presence, and endeavor to inhale the fragrance of the incorruptible Flower, to breathe the sweet savors of holiness, and to obtain a portion of this perfume of celestial glory. Whoso followeth this counsel will break his chains asunder, will taste the abandonment of enraptured love, will attain unto his heart's desire, and will surrender his soul into the hands of his Beloved. Bursting through his cage, he will, even as the bird of the spirit, wing his flight to his holy and everlasting nest.   **31**

Selections from the
Writings of the Báb

Returning to God

In the Presence of God

THIS mortal life is sure to perish; its pleasures are bound to fade away, and erelong ye shall return unto God, distressed with pangs of remorse, for presently ye shall be roused from your slumber, and ye shall soon find yourselves in the presence of God and will be asked of your doings. **32**

The End of Earthly Life

SAY: this earthly life shall come to an end, and everyone shall expire and return unto my Lord God, Who will reward with the choicest gifts the deeds of those who endure with patience. Verily, thy God assigneth the measure of all created things as He willeth, by virtue of His behest; and those who conform to the good-pleasure of your Lord, they are indeed among the blissful. **33**

The Advantageous Life to Come

THE life to come is indeed far more advantageous unto Thee and unto such as follow Thy Cause than this earthly life and its pleasures. This is what hath been foreordained according to the dispensations of Providence. . . . **34**

The Relationship between the Body and the Spirit

As this physical frame is the throne of the inner temple, whatever occurs to the former is felt by the latter. In reality that which takes delight in joy or is saddened by pain is the inner temple of the body, not the body itself. Since this physical body is the throne whereon the inner temple is established, God hath ordained that the body be preserved to the extent possible, so that nothing that causeth repugnance may be experienced. The inner temple beholdeth its physical frame, which is its throne. Thus, if the latter is accorded respect, it is as if the former is the recipient. The converse is likewise true.

Therefore, it hath been ordained that the dead body should be treated with the utmost honor and respect.   35

Returning to God

All men have proceeded from God and unto Him shall all return. All shall appear before Him for judgment. He is the Lord of the Day of Resurrection, of Regeneration and of Reckoning, and His revealed Word is the Balance.   36

The Meaning of Death, Resurrection, and Paradise

True death is realized when a person dieth to himself at the time of His Revelation in such wise that he seeketh naught except Him.

True resurrection from the sepulchres means to be quickened in conformity with His Will, through the power of His utterance.

Paradise is attainment of His good-pleasure and everlasting hell fire His judgment through justice.

The Day He revealeth Himself is Resurrection Day which shall last as long as He ordaineth.   **37**

The Day of Resurrection

THE Day of Resurrection is a day on which the sun riseth and setteth like unto any other day. How oft hath the Day of Resurrection dawned, and the people of the land where it occurred did not learn of the event. Had they heard, they would not have believed, and thus they were not told!   **38**

. . . WHAT is meant by the Day of Resurrection is this, that from the time of the appearance of Him Who is the Tree of divine Reality, at whatever period and under whatever name, until the moment of His disappearance, is the Day of Resurrection.

For example, from the inception of the mission of Jesus—may peace be upon Him—till the day of His ascension was the Resurrection of Moses. For during that period the Revelation of God shone forth through the appearance of that divine Reality, Who rewarded by His Word everyone who believed in Moses, and punished by His Word everyone who did not believe; inasmuch as God's Testimony for that Day was that which

He had solemnly affirmed in the Gospel. And from
the inception of the Revelation of the Apostle of
God—may the blessings of God be upon Him—till
the day of His ascension was the Resurrection of
Jesus—peace be upon Him—wherein the Tree
of divine Reality appeared in the person of
Muḥammad, rewarding by His Word everyone who
was a believer in Jesus, and punishing by His
Word everyone who was not a believer in Him.

39

Paradise and the Means of Its Attainment

Attaining Paradise

No created thing shall ever attain its paradise unless it appeareth in its highest prescribed degree of perfection. For instance, this crystal representeth the paradise of the stone whereof its substance is composed. Likewise there are various stages in the paradise for the crystal itself . . . So long as it was stone it was worthless, but if it attaineth the excellence of ruby—a potentiality which is latent in it—how much a carat will it be worth? Consider likewise every created thing.

Man's highest station, however, is attained through faith in God in every Dispensation and by acceptance of what hath been revealed by Him, and not through learning; inasmuch as in every nation there are learned men who are versed in divers sciences. Nor is it attainable through wealth; for it is similarly evident that among the various classes in every nation there are those possessed of riches. Likewise are other transitory things.

True knowledge, therefore, is the knowledge of God, and this is none other than the recognition of His Manifestation in each Dispensation. Nor is there any wealth save in poverty in all save God and sanctity from aught else but Him—a state that can be realized only when demonstrated towards Him Who is the Dayspring of His Revelation. **40**

The Meaning of Paradise and the Fire

AND know thou of a certainty that by Paradise is meant recognition of and submission unto Him Whom God shall make manifest, and by the fire the company of such souls as would fail to submit unto Him or to be resigned to His good-pleasure.   **41**

Attaining Paradise by Recognizing God's Manifestation

THERE is no paradise more wondrous for any soul than to be exposed to God's Manifestation in His Day, to hear His verses and believe in them, to attain His presence, which is naught but the presence of God, to sail upon the sea of the heavenly kingdom of His good-pleasure, and to partake of the choice fruits of the paradise of His divine Oneness.   **42**

Attaining Paradise by Obedience to God's Commandments

THERE is no paradise, in the estimation of the believers in the divine Unity, more exalted than to obey God's commandments, and there is no fire in the eyes of those who have known God and His signs, fiercer than to transgress His laws and to oppress another soul, even to the extent of a mustard seed. On the Day of Resurrection God will, in truth, judge all men, and we all, verily, plead for His grace.   **43**

Attaining Paradise by Believing in the Divine Words

IN this Day, therefore, I bear witness unto My creatures, for the witness of no one other than Myself hath been or shall ever be worthy of mention in My presence. I affirm that no Paradise is more sublime for My creatures than to stand before My face and to believe in My holy Words, while no fire hath been or will be fiercer for them than to be veiled from the Manifestation of My exalted Self and to disbelieve in My Words. **44**

Striving to Gain Admittance into Paradise

VERILY, on the First Day We flung open the gates of Paradise unto all the peoples of the world, and exclaimed: "O all ye created things! Strive to gain admittance into Paradise, since ye have, during all your lives, held fast unto virtuous deeds in order to attain unto it." Surely all men yearn to enter therein, but alas, they are unable to do so by reason of that which their hands have wrought. Shouldst thou, however, gain a true understanding of God in thine heart of hearts, ere He hath manifested Himself, thou wouldst be able to recognize Him, visible and resplendent, when He unveileth Himself before the eyes of all men. **45**

The Meaning of Life and Death

SAY: the power of God is in the hearts of those who believe in the unity of God and bear witness that no God is there but Him, while the hearts of them that associate partners with God are impotent, devoid of life on this earth, for assuredly they are dead. **46**

The Rewards of the Faithful

The Peace of Attainment

WHENEVER the faithful hear the verses of this Book being recited, their eyes will overflow with tears, and their hearts will be deeply touched by Him Who is the Most Great Remembrance for the love they cherish for God, the All-Praised. He is God, the All-Knowing, the Eternal. They are indeed the inmates of the all-highest Paradise wherein they will abide for ever. Verily, they will see naught therein save that which hath proceeded from God, nothing that will lie beyond the compass of their understanding. There they will meet the believers in Paradise, who will address them with the words "Peace, Peace" lingering on their lips. . . .   47

Everlasting Union

O QURRATU'L-'AYN!* Deliver the summons of the most exalted Word unto the handmaids among Thy kindred, caution them against the Most Great Fire and announce unto them the joyful

_____
*The solace of the eyes, an Arabic literary title of endearment expressing spiritual affection for a beloved one. In this passage it refers to the Báb.

tidings that following this mighty Covenant there
shall be everlasting reunion with God in the
Paradise of His good-pleasure, nigh unto the Seat of
Holiness. Verily, God, the Lord of creation, is
potent over all things.   48

A Promised Reward

VERILY, God shall soon reward thee and those
who have believed in His signs with an
excellent reward from His presence. Assuredly, no
God is there other than Him, the All-Possessing,
the Most Generous. The revelations of His bounty
pervade all created things; He is the Merciful, the
Compassionate.   49

Offerings Preserved

O PEOPLES of the world! Whatsoever ye have
offered up in the way of the One True God,
ye shall indeed find preserved by God, the
Preserver, intact at God's Holy Gate.   50

Selections from the
Writings of 'Abdu'l-Bahá

Proofs of Life after Death

The Immortal Soul

THE whole physical creation is perishable. These material bodies are composed of atoms; when these atoms begin to separate, decomposition sets in; then comes what we call death. This composition of atoms, which constitutes the body or mortal element of any created being, is temporary. When the power of attraction, which holds these atoms together, is withdrawn, the body, as such, ceases to exist.

With the soul it is different. The soul is not a combination of elements; it is not composed of many atoms, it is of one indivisible substance and, therefore, eternal. It is entirely out of the order of the physical creation; it is immortal!

Scientific philosophy has demonstrated that a *simple* element ("simple" meaning "not composed") is indestructible, eternal. The soul, not being a composition of elements, is, in character, as a simple element, and, therefore, cannot cease to exist.

The soul, being of that one indivisible substance, can suffer neither disintegration nor destruction; therefore, there is no reason for its coming to an end. All things living show signs of their existence, and it follows that these signs could not of themselves exist if that which they express or to which they testify had no being.

A thing which does not exist can, of course, give no sign of its existence. The manifold signs of the existence of the spirit are forever before us.

The traces of the Spirit of Jesus Christ, the influence of His divine teaching, is present with us today, and is everlasting.

A nonexistent thing, it is agreed, cannot be seen by signs. In order to write a man must exist— one who does not exist cannot write. Writing is, in itself, a sign of the writer's soul and intelligence. The sacred writings (with ever the same teaching) prove the continuity of the spirit.

Consider the aim of creation: Is it possible that all is created to evolve and develop through countless ages with this small goal in view—a few years of a man's life on earth? Is it not unthinkable that this should be the final aim of existence?

The mineral evolves till it is absorbed in the life of the plant; the plant progresses till finally it loses its life in that of the animal; the animal, in its turn, forming part of the food of man, is absorbed into human life.

Thus, man is shown to be the sum of all creation, the superior of all created beings, the goal to which countless ages of existence have progressed.

At the best, man spends fourscore years and ten in this world—a short time indeed!

Does a man cease to exist when he leaves the body? If his life comes to an end, then all the previous evolution is useless; all has been for nothing! Can one imagine that creation has no greater aim than this?

The soul is eternal, immortal.

Materialists say, "Where is the soul? What is it? We cannot see it, neither can we touch it."

This is how we must answer them: However much the mineral may progress, it cannot comprehend the vegetable world. Now, that lack of comprehension does not prove the nonexistence of the plant!

To however great a degree the plant may have evolved, it is unable to understand the animal world; this ignorance is no proof that the animal does not exist!

The animal, be he never so highly developed, cannot imagine the intelligence of man; neither can he realize the nature of his soul. But, again, this does not prove that man is without intellect, or without soul. It only demonstrates this, that one form of existence is incapable of comprehending a form superior to itself.

This flower may be unconscious of such a being as man, but the fact of its ignorance does not prevent the existence of humanity.

In the same way, if materialists do not believe in the existence of the soul, their unbelief does not prove that there is no such realm as the world of spirit. The very existence of man's intelligence proves his immortality; moreover, darkness proves the presence of light, for without light there would be no shadow. Poverty proves the existence of riches, for without riches how could we measure poverty? Ignorance proves that knowledge exists, for without knowledge how could there be ignorance?

Therefore, the idea of mortality presupposes the existence of immortality—for if there were no life eternal, there would be no way of measuring the life of this world!

If the spirit were not immortal, how could the Manifestations of God endure such terrible trials?

Why did Christ Jesus suffer the fearful death on the cross?

Why did Muḥammad bear persecutions?

Why did the Báb make the supreme sacrifice, and why did Bahá'u'lláh pass the years of His life in prison?

Why should all this suffering have been, if not to prove the everlasting life of the spirit?

Christ suffered; He accepted all His trials because of the immortality of His spirit. If a man reflects, he will understand the spiritual significance of the law of progress—how all moves from the inferior to the superior degree.

It is only a man without intelligence who, after considering these things, can imagine that the great scheme of creation should suddenly cease to progress, that evolution should come to such an inadequate end!

Materialists who reason in this way, and contend that we are unable to *see* the world of spirit, or to perceive the blessings of God, are surely like the animals who have no understanding; having eyes they see not; ears they have, but do not hear. And this lack of sight and hearing is a proof of nothing but their own inferiority, of whom we read in the Qur'án, "They are men who are blind and deaf to the Spirit." They do not use that great gift of God, the power of the understanding, by

which they might see with the eyes of the spirit,
hear with spiritual ears and also comprehend with a
divinely enlightened heart.

The inability of the materialistic mind to grasp
the idea of the life eternal is no proof of the
nonexistence of that life.

The comprehension of that other life depends
on our spiritual birth!

My prayer for you is that your spiritual
faculties and aspirations may daily increase, and that
you will never allow the material senses to veil
from your eyes the glories of the heavenly
illumination.   51

The Immortality of the Spirit

THE logical proof of the immortality of the spirit
is this, that no sign can come from a nonexisting
thing—that is to say, it is impossible that from
absolute nonexistence signs should appear—for the
signs are the consequence of an existence, and the
consequence depends upon the existence of the
principle. So from a nonexisting sun no light can
radiate; from a nonexisting sea no waves appear;
from a nonexisting cloud no rain falls; a nonexisting
tree yields no fruit; a nonexisting man neither
manifests nor produces anything. Therefore, as long
as signs of existence appear, they are a proof that
the possessor of the sign is existent.

Consider that today the Kingdom of Christ
exists. From a nonexisting king how could such
a great kingdom be manifested? How, from a
nonexisting sea, can the waves mount so high?

From a nonexisting garden, how can such fragrant breezes be wafted? Reflect that no effect, no trace, no influence remains of any being after its members are dispersed and its elements are decomposed, whether it be a mineral, a vegetable or an animal. There is only the human reality and the spirit of man which, after the disintegration of the members, dispersing of the particles, and the destruction of the composition, persists and continues to act and to have power.

This question is extremely subtle: Consider it attentively. This is a rational proof which we are giving, so that the wise may weigh it in the balance of reason and justice. But if the human spirit will rejoice and be attracted to the Kingdom of God, if the inner sight becomes opened, and the spiritual hearing strengthened, and the spiritual feelings predominant, he will see the immortality of the spirit as clearly as he sees the sun, and the glad tidings and signs of God will encompass him.   52

Life Here and Hereafter

ALL divine philosophers and men of wisdom and understanding, when observing these endless beings, have considered that in this great and infinite universe all things end in the mineral kingdom, that the outcome of the mineral kingdom is the vegetable kingdom, the outcome of the vegetable kingdom is the animal kingdom and the outcome of the animal kingdom the world of man. The consummation of this limitless universe with all its grandeur and glory hath been man

himself, who in this world of being toileth and
suffereth for a time, with divers ills and pains, and
ultimately disintegrates, leaving no trace and no
fruit after him. Were it so, there is no doubt that
this infinite universe with all its perfections has
ended in sham and delusion with no result, no fruit,
no permanence and no effect. It would be utterly
without meaning. They were thus convinced
that such is not the case, that this great workshop
with all its power, its bewildering magnificence and
endless perfections, cannot eventually come to
naught. That still another life should exist is thus
certain, and, just as the vegetable kingdom is
unaware of the world of man, so we, too, know not
of the great life hereafter that followest the life of
man here below. Our noncomprehension of that
life, however, is no proof of its nonexistence. The
mineral world, for instance, is utterly unaware
of the world of man and cannot comprehend it, but
the ignorance of a thing is no proof of its
nonexistence. Numerous and conclusive proofs exist
that go to show that this infinite world cannot end
with this human life.   53

The Next Life the Fruit of This Life

WHEN thou lookest about thee with a
perceptive eye, thou wilt note that on this
dusty earth all humankind are suffering. . . . And if
a human life, with its spiritual being, were
limited to this earthly span, then what would be the
harvest of creation? Indeed, what would be the
effects and the outcomes of Divinity Itself? Were

such a notion true, then all created things, all
contingent realities, and this whole world of
being—all would be meaningless. God forbid that
one should hold to such a fiction and gross error.

For just as the effects and the fruitage of
the uterine life are not to be found in that dark and
narrow place, and only when the child is transferred
to this wide earth do the benefits and uses of
growth and development in that previous world
become revealed—so likewise reward and
punishment, heaven and hell, requital and
retribution for actions done in this present life, will
stand revealed in that other world beyond. And
just as, if human life in the womb were limited to
that uterine world, existence there would be
nonsensical, irrelevant—so too if the life of this
world, the deeds here done and their fruitage, did
not come forth in the world beyond, the whole
process would be irrational and foolish.

Know, then, that the Lord God possesseth
invisible realms which the human intellect
can never hope to fathom nor the mind of man
conceive. When once thou hast cleansed the
channel of thy spiritual sense from the pollution of
this worldly life, then wilt thou breathe in the
sweet scents of holiness that blow from the blissful
bowers of that heavenly land.   54

The Soul—The True Reality

The Reality of Humankind

M AN—the true man—is soul, not body; though physically man belongs to the animal kingdom, yet his soul lifts him above the rest of creation. Behold how the light of the sun illuminates the world of matter: Even so doth the divine light shed its rays in the kingdom of the soul. The soul it is which makes the human creature a celestial entity!

By the power of the Holy Spirit, working through his soul, man is able to perceive the divine reality of things. All great works of art and science are witnesses to this power of the Spirit.

The same Spirit gives eternal life.   55

The Sum of All Creation

T HE superiority of man over the rest of the created world is seen again in this, that man has a soul in which dwells the divine spirit; the souls of the lower creatures are inferior in their essence.

There is no doubt, then, that of all created beings man is the nearest to the nature of God and, therefore, receives a greater gift of the divine bounty.

The mineral kingdom possesses the power of

existing. The plant has the power of existing and growing. The animal, in addition to existence and growth, has the capacity of moving about, and the use of the faculties of the senses. In the human kingdom we find all the attributes of the lower worlds, with much more added thereto. Man is the sum of every previous creation, for he contains them all.

To man is given the special gift of the intellect by which he is able to receive a larger share of the light divine. The Perfect Man is as a polished mirror reflecting the Sun of Truth, manifesting the attributes of God.   56

The Relationship of the Body and the Soul

SOME think that the body is the substance and exists by itself, and that the spirit is accidental and depends upon the substance of the body, although, on the contrary, the rational soul is the substance, and the body depends upon it. If the accident—that is to say, the body—be destroyed, the substance, the spirit, remains.

Second, the rational soul, meaning the human spirit, does not descend into the body—that is to say, it does not enter it, for descent and entrance are characteristics of bodies, and the rational soul is exempt from this. The spirit never entered this body, so in quitting it, it will not be in need of an abiding-place: No, the spirit is connected with the body, as this light is with this mirror. When the mirror is clear and perfect, the light of the lamp will be apparent in it, and when the mirror becomes

covered with dust or breaks, the light will
disappear.

The rational soul—that is to say, the human
spirit—has neither entered this body nor existed
through it; so after the disintegration of the
composition of the body, how should it be in need
of a substance through which it may exist? On
the contrary, the rational soul is the substance
through which the body exists. The personality of
the rational soul is from its beginning; it is not
due to the instrumentality of the body, but the state
and the personality of the rational soul may be
strengthened in this world; it will make progress
and will attain to the degrees of perfection, or
it will remain in the lowest abyss of ignorance,
veiled and deprived from beholding the signs of
God.   57

The Beginning of the Human Soul

KNOW that, although the human soul has existed
on the earth for prolonged times and ages,
yet it is phenomenal.* As it is a divine sign, when
once it has come into existence, it is eternal.
The spirit of man has a beginning, but it has no
end; it continues eternally. In the same way
the species existing on this earth are phenomenal,
for it is established that there was a time when these
species did not exist on the surface of the earth.
Moreover, the earth has not always existed, but the

---

*i.e., at its birth.

world of existence has always been, for the
universe is not limited to this terrestrial globe. The
meaning of this is that, although human souls are
phenomenal, they are nevertheless immortal,
everlasting and perpetual; for the world of things is
the world of imperfection in comparison with
that of man, and the world of man is the world of
perfection in comparison with that of things. When
imperfections reach the station of perfection, they
become eternal.* This is an example of which
you must comprehend the meaning.   **58**

The Power and the Potential of a Pure Soul

SOULS are like unto mirrors, and the bounty of
God is like unto the sun. When the mirrors pass
beyond all coloring and attain purity and polish,
and are confronted with the sun, they will reflect in
full perfection its light and glory. In this condition
one should not consider the mirror, but the
power of the light of the sun, which hath penetrated
the mirror, making it a reflector of the heavenly
glory.   **59**

The Relationship between Body, Soul, and Spirit

THERE are in the world of humanity three
degrees—those of the body, the soul, and spirit.
The body is the physical or animal degree of

---

*i.e., in the kingdom of man, where alone the spirit
manifests immortality.

man. From the bodily point of view man is a sharer
of the animal kingdom. The bodies alike of men
and animals are composed of elements held together
by the law of attraction.

Like the animal, man possesses the faculties of
the senses, is subject to heat, cold, hunger, thirst,
etc.; unlike the animal, man has a rational soul, the
human intelligence.

This intelligence of man is the intermediary
between his body and his spirit.

When man allows the spirit, through his soul,
to enlighten his understanding, then does he
contain all creation, because man, being the
culmination of all that went before and thus superior
to all previous evolutions, contains all the lower
world within himself. Illumined by the spirit
through the instrumentality of the soul, man's
radiant intelligence makes him the crowning-point
of creation.

But, on the other hand, when man does not
open his mind and heart to the blessing of the
spirit, but turns his soul towards the material side,
towards the bodily part of his nature, then is he
fallen from his high place, and he becomes inferior
to the inhabitants of the lower animal kingdom.
In this case the man is in a sorry plight! For if the
spiritual qualities of the soul, open to the breath of
the divine Spirit, are never used, they become
atrophied, enfeebled, and at last incapable, whilst
the soul's material qualities alone being exercised,
they become terribly powerful—and the unhappy,
misguided man, becomes more savage, more unjust,
more vile, more cruel, more malevolent than the
lower animals themselves. All his aspirations

and desires being strengthened by the lower side of
the soul's nature, he becomes more and more brutal,
until his whole being is in no way superior to that
of the beasts that perish. Men such as this plan
to work evil, to hurt and to destroy; they are
entirely without the spirit of divine compassion, for
the celestial quality of the soul has been dominated
by that of the material. If, on the contrary, the
spiritual nature of the soul has been so strengthened
that it holds the material side in subjection, then
does the man approach the divine; his humanity
becomes so glorified that the virtues of the Celestial
Assembly are manifested in him; he radiates the
mercy of God, he stimulates the spiritual progress
of mankind, for he becomes a lamp to show
light on their path.

You perceive how the soul is the intermediary
between the body and the spirit. In like manner is
this tree* the intermediary between the seed and
the fruit. When the fruit of the tree appears
and becomes ripe, then we know that the tree is
perfect; if the tree bore no fruit, it would be merely
a useless growth, serving no purpose!

When a soul has in it the life of the spirit,
then does it bring forth good fruit and become a
divine tree. I wish you to try to understand this
example. I hope that the unspeakable goodness of
God will so strengthen you that the celestial quality
of your soul, which relates it to the spirit, will
forever dominate the material side, so entirely
ruling the senses that your soul will approach the

------

*A small orange tree on the table nearby.

perfections of the heavenly Kingdom. May your
faces, being steadfastly set towards the divine light,
become so luminous that all your thoughts, words
and actions will shine with the spiritual radiance
dominating your souls, so that in the gatherings of
the world you will show perfection in your life.

Some men's lives are solely occupied with the
things of this world; their minds are so
circumscribed by exterior manners and traditional
interests that they are blind to any other realm of
existence, to the spiritual significance of all things!
They think and dream of earthly fame, of
material progress. Sensuous delights and
comfortable surroundings bound their horizon,
their highest ambitions center in successes of
worldly conditions and circumstances! They curb
not their lower propensities; they eat, drink, and
sleep! Like the animal, they have no thought
beyond their own physical well-being. It is true that
these necessities must be despatched. Life is a load
which must be carried on while we are on earth,
but the cares of the lower things of life should not
be allowed to monopolize all the thoughts and
aspirations of a human being. The heart's ambitions
should ascend to a more glorious goal; mental
activity should rise to higher levels! Men should
hold in their souls the vision of celestial perfection,
and there prepare a dwelling-place for the
inexhaustible bounty of the divine spirit.

Let your ambition be the achievement on earth
of a heavenly civilization! I ask for you the
supreme blessing, that you may be so filled with the
vitality of the heavenly spirit that you may be the
cause of life to the world.   **60**

The Difference between Mind, Soul, and Spirit

Question.—*What is the difference between the mind, spirit and soul?* ...

Answer.— ... THE human spirit which distinguishes man from the animal is the rational soul, and these two names—the human spirit and the rational soul—designate one thing.* This spirit, which in the terminology of the philosophers is the rational soul, embraces all beings, and as far as human ability permits discovers the realities of things and becomes cognizant of their peculiarities and effects, and of the qualities and properties of beings. But the human spirit, unless assisted by the spirit of faith, does not become acquainted with the divine secrets and the heavenly realities. It is like a mirror which, although clear, polished and brilliant, is still in need of light. Until

---

*"When studying at present, in English, the available Bahá'í writings on the subject of body, soul and spirit, one is handicapped by a certain lack of clarity because not all were translated by the same person, and also there are, as you know, still many Bahá'í writings untranslated. But there is no doubt that spirit and soul seem to have been interchanged in meaning sometimes; soul and mind have, likewise, been interchanged in meaning, no doubt due to difficulties arising from different translations. What the Bahá'ís do believe though is that we have three aspects of our humanness, so to speak, a body, a mind and an immortal identity—soul or spirit. We believe the mind forms a link between the soul and the body, and the two interact on each other." (Shoghi Effendi, through his secretary, 7 June 1946, in *Arohanui: Letters from Shoghi Effendi to New Zealand* [Fiji: Bahá'í Publishing Trust, 1982], p. 89.)

a ray of the sun reflects upon it, it cannot discover
the heavenly secrets.

But the mind is the power of the human spirit.
Spirit is the lamp; mind is the light which shines
from the lamp. Spirit is the tree, and the mind is the
fruit. Mind is the perfection of the spirit and is its
essential quality, as the sun's rays are the essential
necessity of the sun.   **61**

The Faculties of the Mind and the Soul

Now regarding the question whether the
faculties of the mind and the human soul are
one and the same. These faculties are but the
inherent properties of the soul, such as the power of
imagination, of thought, of understanding—
powers that are the essential requisites of the reality
of man, even as the solar ray is the inherent
property of the sun. The temple of man is like unto
a mirror, his soul is as the sun, and his mental
faculties even as the rays that emanate from that
source of light. The ray may cease to fall upon the
mirror, but it can in no wise be dissociated from the
sun.   **62**

The Superiority of Human Powers

Now concerning mental faculties, they are in
truth of the inherent properties of the
soul, even as the radiation of light is the essential
property of the sun. The rays of the sun are
renewed, but the sun itself is ever the same and
unchanged. Consider how the human intellect

develops and weakens, and may at times come to
naught, whereas the soul changeth not. For the
mind to manifest itself, the human body must be
whole; and a sound mind cannot be but in a sound
body, whereas the soul dependeth not upon the
body. It is through the power of the soul that the
mind comprehendeth, imagineth and exerteth
its influence, whilst the soul is a power that is free.
The mind comprehendeth the abstract by the aid
of the concrete, but the soul hath limitless
manifestations of its own. The mind is
circumscribed, the soul limitless. It is by the aid of
such senses as those of sight, hearing, taste, smell
and touch that the mind comprehendeth, whereas
the soul is free from all agencies. The soul as
thou observest, whether it be in sleep or waking, is
in motion and ever active. Possibly it may, whilst
in a dream, unravel an intricate problem, incapable
of solution in the waking state. The mind,
moreover, understandeth not whilst the senses have
ceased to function, and in the embryonic stage
and in early infancy the reasoning power is totally
absent, whereas the soul is ever endowed with
full strength. In short, the proofs are many that go
to show that despite the loss of reason, the power of
the soul would still continue to exist. The spirit
however possesseth various grades and stations.

63

Independence of the Soul from the Body

GOD, in His bounty, has given us a foretaste here,
has given us certain proofs of the difference
that exists between body, soul and spirit.

We see that cold, heat, suffering, etc., only concern the *body*; they do not touch the spirit.

How often do we see a man, poor, sick, miserably clad, and with no means of support, yet spiritually strong. Whatever his body has to suffer, his spirit is free and well! Again, how often do we see a rich man, physically strong and healthy, but with a soul sick unto death.

It is quite apparent to the seeing mind that a man's spirit is something very different from his physical body.

The spirit is changeless, indestructible. The progress and development of the soul, the joy and sorrow of the soul, are independent of the physical body.

If we are caused joy or pain by a friend, if a love prove true or false, it is the soul that is affected. If our dear ones are far from us—it is the soul that grieves, and the grief or trouble of the soul may react on the body.

Thus, when the spirit is fed with holy virtues, then is the body joyous; if the soul falls into sin, the body is in torment!

When we find truth, constancy, fidelity, and love, we are happy; but if we meet with lying, faithlessness, and deceit, we are miserable.

These are all things pertaining to the soul, and are not *bodily* ills. Thus it is apparent that the soul, even as the body, has its own individuality. But if the body undergoes a change, the spirit need not be touched. When you break a glass on which the sun shines, the glass is broken, but the sun still shines! If a cage containing a bird is destroyed, the bird is unharmed! If a lamp is broken, the flame can still burn bright!

The same thing applies to the spirit of man. Though death destroy his body, it has no power over his spirit—this is eternal, everlasting, both birthless and deathless.   **64**

The Reality of Thought

THE reality of man is his thought, not his material body. The thought force and the animal force are partners. Although man is part of the animal creation, he possesses a power of thought superior to all other created beings.   **65**

The Soul's Two Modes of Perception

SPIRIT cannot be perceived by the material senses of the physical body, excepting as it is expressed in outward signs and works. The human body is visible; the soul is invisible. It is the soul, nevertheless, that directs a man's faculties, that governs his humanity.

The soul has two main faculties. *(a)* As outer circumstances are communicated to the soul by the eyes, ears, and brain of a man, so does the soul communicate its desires and purposes through the brain to the hands and tongue of the physical body, thereby expressing itself. The spirit in the soul is the very essence of life. *(b)* The second faculty of the soul expresses itself in the world of vision, where the soul inhabited by the spirit has its

being, and functions without the help of the
material bodily senses. There, in the realm of
vision, the soul sees without the help of the physical
eye, hears without the aid of the physical ear, and
travels without dependence upon physical motion.
It is, therefore, clear that the spirit in the soul of
man can function through the physical body
by using the organs of the ordinary senses, and that
it is able also to live and act without their aid in
the world of vision. This proves without a doubt
the superiority of the soul of man over his body, the
superiority of spirit over matter.

For example, look at this lamp: Is not the light
within it superior to the lamp which holds it?
However beautiful the form of the lamp may be, if
the light is not there, its purpose is unfulfilled; it
is without life—a dead thing. The lamp needs the
light, but the light does not need the lamp.

The spirit does not need a body, but the body
needs spirit, or it cannot live. The soul can live
without a body, but the body without a soul dies.

If a man lose his sight, his hearing, his hand or
his foot, should his soul still inhabit the body he
lives, and is able to manifest divine virtues. On the
other hand, without the spirit it would be
impossible for a perfect body to exist. 66

KNOW that the power and the comprehension of
the human spirit are of two kinds—that is
to say, they perceive and act in two different modes.
One way is through instruments and organs: Thus
with this eye it sees; with this ear it hears; with this
tongue it talks. Such is the action of the spirit, and

the perception of the reality of man, by means of organs—that is to say, that the spirit is the seer, through the eyes; the spirit is the hearer, through the ear; the spirit is the speaker, through the tongue.

The other manifestation of the powers and actions of the spirit is without instruments and organs. For example, in the state of sleep without eyes it sees; without an ear it hears; without a tongue it speaks; without feet it runs. Briefly, these actions are beyond the means of instruments and organs. How often it happens that it sees a dream in the world of sleep, and its signification becomes apparent two years afterward in corresponding events. In the same way, how many times it happens that a question which one cannot solve in the world of wakefulness is solved in the world of dreams. In wakefulness the eye sees only for a short distance, but in dreams he who is in the East sees the West. Awake he sees the present; in sleep he sees the future. In wakefulness, by means of rapid transit, at the most he can travel only twenty farsakhs* an hour; in sleep, in the twinkling of an eye, he traverses the East and West. For the spirit travels in two different ways: without means, which is spiritual traveling; and with means, which is material traveling: as birds which fly, and those which are carried.

In the time of sleep this body is as though dead; it does not see nor hear; it does not feel; it has no consciousness, no perception—that is to say,

_____
*One *farsakh* is equivalent to about four miles.

the powers of man have become inactive, but the
spirit lives and subsists. Nay, its penetration is
increased, its flight is higher, and its intelligence is
greater. To consider that after the death of the
body the spirit perishes is like imagining that a bird
in a cage will be destroyed if the cage is broken,
though the bird has nothing to fear from the
destruction of the cage. Our body is like the cage,
and the spirit is like the bird. We see that without
the cage this bird flies in the world of sleep;
therefore, if the cage becomes broken, the bird will
continue and exist. Its feelings will be even more
powerful, its perceptions greater, and its happiness
increased. In truth, from hell it reaches a paradise of
delights because for the thankful birds there is no
paradise greater than freedom from the cage. That
is why with utmost joy and happiness the martyrs
hasten to the plain of sacrifice.

In wakefulness the eye of man sees at the
utmost as far as one hour of distance* because
through the instrumentality of the body the power
of the spirit is thus determined; but with the
inner sight and the mental eye it sees America, and
it can perceive that which is there, and discover
the conditions of things and organize affairs.
If, then, the spirit were the same as the body, it
would be necessary that the power of the inner sight
should also be in the same proportion. Therefore,
it is evident that this spirit is different from the
body, and that the bird is different from the cage,
and that the power and penetration of the spirit
is stronger without the intermediary of the body. 67

*It is a Persian custom to reckon distance by time.

The Voice Within

WHEN you wish to reflect upon or consider a matter, you consult something within you. You say, shall I do it, or shall I not do it? Is it better to make this journey or abandon it? Whom do you consult? Who is within you deciding this question? Surely there is a distinct power, an intelligent ego. Were it not distinct from your ego, you would not be consulting it. It is greater than the faculty of thought. It is your spirit which teaches you, which advises and decides upon matters. Who is it that interrogates? Who is it that answers? There is no doubt that it is the spirit and that there is no change or transformation in it, for it is not a composition of elements, and anything that is not composed of elements is eternal. Change and transformation are peculiarities of composition. There is no change and transformation in the spirit. In proof of this, the body may become weakened in its members. It may be dismembered, or one of its members may be incapacitated. The whole body may be paralyzed; and yet the mind, the spirit, remains ever the same. The mind decides; the thought is perfect; and yet the hand is withered, the feet have become useless, the spinal column is paralyzed, and there is no muscular movement at all, but the spirit is in the same status. Dismember a healthy man; the spirit is not dismembered. Amputate his feet; his spirit is there. He may become lame; the spirit is not affected. The spirit is ever the same; no change or transformation can you perceive, and because there is no change or transformation, it is everlasting and permanent.

Consider a man while in the state of sleep; it is evident that all his parts and members are at a standstill, are functionless. His eye does not see, his ear does not hear, his feet and hands are motionless; but, nevertheless, he does see in the world of dreams, he does hear, he speaks, he walks, he may even fly in an airplane. Therefore, it becomes evident that though the body be dead, yet the spirit is alive and permanent. Nay, the perceptions may be keener when man's body is asleep, the flight may be higher, the hearing may be more acute; all the functions are there, and yet the body is at a standstill. Hence it is proof that there is a spirit in the man, and in this spirit there is no distinction as to whether the body be asleep or absolutely dead and dependent. The spirit is not incapacitated by these conditions; it is not bereft of its existence; it is not bereft of its perfections. The proofs are many, innumerable.

These are all rational proofs. Nobody can refute them. As we have shown that there is a spirit and that this spirit is permanent and everlasting, we must strive to learn of it. May you become informed of its power, hasten to render it divine, to have it become sanctified and holy and make it the very light of the world illumining the East and the West. 68

Spiritual Discoveries

THOU didst write as to the question of spiritual discoveries. The spirit of man is a circumambient power that encompasseth the realities of all things. Whatsoever thou dost see

about thee—wondrous products of human
workmanship, inventions, discoveries and like
evidences—each one of these was once a secret
hidden away in the realm of the unknown.
The human spirit laid that secret bare, and drew it
forth from the unseen into the visible world. There
is, for example, the power of steam, and
photography and the phonograph, and wireless
telegraphy, and advances in mathematics: Each and
every one of these was once a mystery, a closely
guarded secret, yet the human spirit unravelled
these secrets and brought them out of the invisible
into the light of day. Thus it is clear that the human
spirit is an all-encompassing power that exerteth
its dominion over the inner essences of all created
things, uncovering the well-kept mysteries of
the phenomenal world.

The divine spirit, however, doth unveil divine
realities and universal mysteries that lie within
the spiritual world. It is my hope that thou
wilt attain unto this divine spirit, so that thou
mayest uncover the secrets of the other world, as
well as the mysteries of the world below.   **69**

Visions and Communication with Spirits

REFLECT that man's power of thought consists of
two kinds. One kind is true, when it agrees
with a determined truth. Such conceptions find
realization in the exterior world; such are accurate
opinions, correct theories, scientific discoveries and
inventions.

The other kind of conceptions is made up of

vain thoughts and useless ideas which yield neither
fruit nor result, and which have no reality. No,
they surge like the waves of the sea of imaginations,
and they pass away like idle dreams.

In the same way, there are two sorts of
spiritual discoveries. One is the revelations of the
Prophets, and the spiritual discoveries of the elect.
The visions of the Prophets are not dreams; no,
they are spiritual discoveries and have reality. They
say, for example, "I saw a person in a certain
form, and I said such a thing, and he gave such an
answer." This vision is in the world of wakefulness,
and not in that of sleep. Nay, it is a spiritual
discovery which is expressed as if it were the
appearance of a vision.

The other kind of spiritual discoveries is made
up of pure imaginations, but these imaginations
become embodied in such a way that many simple-
hearted people believe that they have a reality.
That which proves it clearly is that from this
controlling of spirits no result or fruit has ever been
produced. No, they are but narratives and stories.

Know that the reality of man embraces the
realities of things, and discovers the verities,
properties and secrets of things. So all these arts,
wonders, sciences and knowledge have been
discovered by the human reality. At one time these
sciences, knowledge, wonders and arts were hidden
and concealed secrets; then gradually the human
reality discovered them and brought them from the
realm of the invisible to the plane of the visible.
Therefore, it is evident that the reality of man
embraces things. Thus it is in Europe and discovers
America; it is on the earth, and it makes discoveries

in the heavens. It is the revealer of the secrets of things, and it is the knower of the realities of that which exists. These discoveries corresponding to the reality are similar to revelation, which is spiritual comprehension, divine inspiration and the association of human spirits. For instance, the Prophet says, "I saw, I said, I heard such a thing." It is, therefore, evident that the spirit has great perception without the intermediary of any of the five senses, such as the eyes or ears. Among spiritual souls there are spiritual understandings, discoveries, a communion which is purified from imagination and fancy, an association which is sanctified from time and place. So it is written in the Gospel that, on Mount Tabor, Moses and Elias came to Christ, and it is evident that this was not a material meeting. It was a spiritual condition which is expressed as a physical meeting.

The other sort of converse, presence and communications of spirits is but imagination and fancy, which only appears to have reality.

The mind and the thought of man sometimes discover truths, and from this thought and discovery signs and results are produced. This thought has a foundation. But many things come to the mind of man which are like the waves of the sea of imaginations; they have no fruit, and no result comes from them. In the same way, man sees in the world of sleep a vision which becomes exactly realized; at another time, he sees a dream which has absolutely no result.

What we mean is that this state, which we call the converse and communications of spirits, is of two kinds: One is simply imaginary, and the other

is like the visions which are mentioned in the Holy
Book, such as the revelations of St. John and
Isaiah and the meeting of Christ with Moses and
Elias. These are real, and produce wonderful effects
in the minds and thoughts of men, and cause their
hearts to be attracted. 70

The Soul's Progress and Condition
in This World and the Next

Entrance into the Kingdom of God

YOU question about eternal life and the entrance into the Kingdom. The outer expression used for the Kingdom is heaven; but this is a comparison and similitude, not a reality or fact, for the Kingdom is not a material place; it is sanctified from time and place. It is a spiritual world, a divine world, and the center of the Sovereignty of God; it is freed from body and that which is corporeal, and it is purified and sanctified from the imaginations of the human world. To be limited to place is a property of bodies and not of spirits. Place and time surround the body, not the mind and spirit. Observe that the body of man is confined to a small place; it covers only two spans of earth. But the spirit and mind of man travel to all countries and regions—even through the limitless space of the heavens—surround all that exists, and make discoveries in the exalted spheres and infinite distances. This is because the spirit has no place; it is placeless; and for the spirit the earth and the heaven are as one since it makes discoveries in both. But the body is limited to a place and does not know that which is beyond it.

For life is of two kinds: that of the body and
that of the spirit. The life of the body is material
life, but the life of the spirit expresses the existence
of the Kingdom, which consists in receiving the
Spirit of God and becoming vivified by the breath
of the Holy Spirit. Although the material life
has existence, it is pure nonexistence and absolute
death for the holy saints. So man exists, and this
stone also exists, but what a difference between the
existence of man and that of the stone! Though
the stone exists, in relation to the existence of man
it is nonexistent.

The meaning of eternal life is the gift of the
Holy Spirit, as the flower receives the gift of the
season, the air, and the breezes of spring. Consider:
This flower had life in the beginning like the life
of the mineral; but by the coming of the season of
spring, of the bounty of the clouds of the
springtime, and of the heat of the glowing sun, it
attained to another life of the utmost freshness,
delicacy and fragrance. The first life of the flower,
in comparison to the second life, is death.

The meaning is that the life of the Kingdom is
the life of the spirit, the eternal life, and that it is
purified from place, like the spirit of man which has
no place. For if you examine the human body, you
will not find a special spot or locality for the
spirit, for it has never had a place; it is immaterial.
It has a connection with the body like that of the
sun with this mirror. The sun is not within the
mirror, but it has a connection with the mirror.

In the same way the world of the Kingdom is
sanctified from everything that can be perceived

by the eye or by the other senses—hearing, smell, taste or touch. The mind which is in man, the existence of which is recognized—where is it in him? If you examine the body with the eye, the ear or the other senses, you will not find it; nevertheless, it exists. Therefore, the mind has no place, but it is connected with the brain. The Kingdom is also like this. In the same way love has no place, but it is connected with the heart; so the Kingdom has no place, but is connected with man.

Entrance into the Kingdom is through the love of God, through detachment, through holiness and chastity, through truthfulness, purity, steadfastness, faithfulness and the sacrifice of life.

These explanations show that man is immortal and lives eternally. For those who believe in God, who have love of God, and faith, life is excellent— that is, it is eternal; but to those souls who are veiled from God, although they have life, it is dark, and in comparison with the life of believers it is nonexistence.

For example, the eye and the nail are living; but the life of the nail in relation to the life of the eye is nonexistent. This stone and this man both exist; but the stone in relation to the existence of man is nonexistent; it has no being; for when man dies, and his body is destroyed and annihilated, it becomes like stone and earth. Therefore, it is clear that although the mineral exists, in relation to man it is nonexistent.

In the same way, the souls who are veiled from God, although they exist in this world and in the world after death, are, in comparison with the holy

existence of the children of the Kingdom of God,
nonexisting and separated from God.   **71**

The Kingdom of Heaven

O THOU who seekest the Kingdom of heaven!
This world is even as the body of man,
and the Kingdom of God is as the spirit of life. See
how dark and narrow is the physical world of
man's body, and what a prey it is to diseases and ills.
On the other hand, how fresh and bright is the
realm of the human spirit. Judge thou from this
metaphor how the world of the Kingdom hath
shone down, and how its laws have been made to
work in this nether realm. Although the spirit
is hidden from view, still its commandments shine
out like rays of light upon the world of the
human body. In the same way, although the
Kingdom of heaven is hidden from the sight of this
unwitting people, still, to him who seeth with the
inner eye, it is plain as day.

Wherefore dwell thou ever in the Kingdom,
and be thou oblivious of this world below. Be thou
so wholly absorbed in the emanations of the
spirit that nothing in the world of man will distract
thee.   **72**

T HE souls of the children of the Kingdom, after
their separation from the body, ascend unto
the realm of everlasting life. But if ye ask as to the
place, know ye that the world of existence is a
single world, although its stations are various and

distinct. For example, the mineral life occupieth its own plane, but a mineral entity is without any awareness at all of the vegetable kingdom, and, indeed, with its inner tongue denieth that there is any such kingdom. In the same way, a vegetable entity knoweth nothing of the animal world, remaining completely heedless and ignorant thereof, for the stage of the animal is higher than that of the vegetable, and the vegetable is veiled from the animal world and inwardly denieth the existence of that world—all this while animal, vegetable and mineral dwell together in the one world. In the same way the animal remaineth totally unaware of that power of the human mind which graspeth universal ideas and layeth bare the secrets of creation—so that a man who liveth in the East can make plans and arrangements for the West; can unravel mysteries; although located on the continent of Europe can discover America; although sited on the earth can lay hold of the inner realities of the stars of heaven. Of this power of discovery which belongeth to the human mind, this power which can grasp abstract and universal ideas, the animal remaineth totally ignorant, and indeed denieth its existence.

     In the same way, the denizens of this earth are completely unaware of the world of the Kingdom and deny the existence thereof. They ask, for example: "Where is the Kingdom? Where is the Lord of the Kingdom?" These people are even as the mineral and the vegetable, who know nothing whatever of the animal and the human realm; they see it not; they find it not. Yet the

mineral and vegetable, the animal and man, are all
living here together in this world of existence.   73

Attributes Necessary for Entering
the Kingdom of Heaven

IN the world of existence man has traversed
successive degrees until he has attained the
human kingdom. In each degree of his progression
he has developed capacity for advancement to the
next station and condition. While in the kingdom
of the mineral he was attaining the capacity for
promotion into the degree of the vegetable. In the
kingdom of the vegetable he underwent preparation
for the world of the animal, and from thence he
has come onward to the human degree, or
kingdom. Throughout this journey of progression
he has ever and always been potentially man.

In the beginning of his human life man was
embryonic in the world of the matrix. There he
received capacity and endowment for the reality of
human existence. The forces and powers necessary
for this world were bestowed upon him in that
limited condition. In this world he needed eyes; he
received them potentially in the other. He needed
ears; he obtained them there in readiness and
preparation for his new existence. The powers
requisite in this world were conferred upon him in
the world of the matrix so that when he entered
this realm of real existence he not only possessed all
necessary functions and powers but found provision
for his material sustenance awaiting him.

Therefore, in this world he must prepare himself for the life beyond. That which he needs in the world of the Kingdom must be obtained here. Just as he prepared himself in the world of the matrix by acquiring forces necessary in this sphere of existence, so, likewise, the indispensable forces of the divine existence must be potentially attained in this world.

What is he in need of in the Kingdom which transcends the life and limitation of this mortal sphere? That world beyond is a world of sanctity and radiance; therefore, it is necessary that in this world he should acquire these divine attributes. In that world there is need of spirituality, faith, assurance, the knowledge and love of God. These he must attain in this world so that after his ascension from the earthly to the heavenly Kingdom he shall find all that is needful in that eternal life ready for him.

That divine world is manifestly a world of lights; therefore, man has need of illumination here. That is a world of love; the love of God is essential. It is a world of perfections; virtues, or perfections must be acquired. That world is vivified by the breaths of the Holy Spirit; in this world we must seek them. That is the Kingdom of everlasting life; it must be attained during this vanishing existence.

By what means can man acquire these things? How shall he obtain these merciful gifts and powers? First, through the knowledge of God. Second, through the love of God. Third, through faith. Fourth, through philanthropic deeds. Fifth, through self-sacrifice. Sixth, through severance from this world. Seventh, through sanctity

and holiness. Unless he acquires these forces and
attains to these requirements, he will surely be
deprived of the life that is eternal. But if he
possesses the knowledge of God, becomes ignited
through the fire of the love of God, witnesses
the great and mighty signs of the Kingdom,
becomes the cause of love among mankind and lives
in the utmost state of sanctity and holiness, he
shall surely attain to second birth, be baptized by
the Holy Spirit and enjoy everlasting existence.

Is it not astonishing that although man has
been created for the knowledge and love of God, for
the virtues of the human world, for spirituality,
heavenly illumination and eternal life, nevertheless,
he continues ignorant and negligent of all this?
Consider how he seeks knowledge of everything
except knowledge of God. For instance, his utmost
desire is to penetrate the mysteries of the lowest
strata of the earth. Day by day he strives to know
what can be found ten meters below the surface,
what he can discover within the stone, what he can
learn by archaeological research in the dust. He puts
forth arduous labors to fathom terestrial mysteries
but is not at all concerned about knowing the
mysteries of the Kingdom, traversing the illimitable
fields of the eternal world, becoming informed of
the divine realities, discovering the secrets of God,
attaining the knowledge of God, witnessing the
splendors of the Sun of Truth and realizing the
glories of everlasting life. He is unmindful
and thoughtless of these. How much he is attracted
to the mysteries of matter, and how completely
unaware he is of the mysteries of Divinity! Nay, he
is utterly negligent and oblivious of the secrets of

Divinity. How great his ignorance! How conducive
to his degradation! It is as if a kind and loving father
had provided a library of wonderful books for his
son in order that he might be informed of the
mysteries of creation, at the same time surrounding
him with every means of comfort and enjoyment,
but the son amuses himself with pebbles and
playthings, neglectful of all his father's gifts and
provision. How ignorant and heedless is man! The
Father has willed for him eternal glory, and he is
content with blindness and deprivation. The Father
has built for him a royal palace, but he is playing
with the dust; prepared for him garments of
silk, but he prefers to remain unclothed; provided
for him delicious foods and fruits, while he
seeks sustenance in the grasses of the field.   74

Punishments and Rewards

Now punishments and rewards are said to be of
two kinds: first, the rewards and punishments
of this life; second, those of the other world. But
the paradise and hell of existence are found in
all the worlds of God, whether in this world or in
the spiritual, heavenly worlds. Gaining these
rewards is the gaining of eternal life. That is why
Christ said, "Act in such a way that you may
find eternal life, and that you may be born of water
and the spirit, so that you may enter into the
Kingdom."*

---

*Cf. John 3:5.

The rewards of this life are the virtues and
perfections which adorn the reality of man.
For example, he was dark and becomes luminous;
he was ignorant and becomes wise; he was
neglectful and becomes vigilant; he was asleep and
becomes awakened; he was dead and becomes
living; he was blind and becomes a seer; he was deaf
and becomes a hearer; he was earthly and becomes
heavenly; he was material and becomes spiritual.
Through these rewards he gains spiritual birth and
becomes a new creature. He becomes the
manifestation of the verse in the Gospel where it is
said of the disciples that they "were born, not of
blood, nor of the will of the flesh, nor of the will of
man, but of God"*—that is to say, they were
delivered from the animal characteristics and
qualities which are the characteristics of human
nature, and they became qualified with the divine
characteristics, which are the bounty of God. This
is the meaning of the second birth. For such people
there is no greater torture than being veiled from
God, and no more severe punishment than sensual
vices, dark qualities, lowness of nature, engrossment
in carnal desires. When they are delivered through
the light of faith from the darkness of these vices,
and become illuminated with the radiance of the
sun of reality, and ennobled with all the virtues,
they esteem this the greatest reward, and they know
it to be the true paradise. In the same way they
consider that the spiritual punishment—that is to
say, the torture and punishment of existence—is to

---

*John 1:13.

be subjected to the world of nature; to be veiled
from God; to be brutal and ignorant; to fall
into carnal lusts; to be absorbed in animal frailties;
to be characterized with dark qualities, such as
falsehood, tyranny, cruelty, attachment to the affairs
of the world, and being immersed in satanic ideas.
For them, these are the greatest punishments and
tortures.

Likewise, the rewards of the other world are
the eternal life which is clearly mentioned in all the
Holy Books, the divine perfections, the eternal
bounties and everlasting felicity. The rewards of the
other world are the perfections and the peace
obtained in the spiritual worlds after leaving this
world, while the rewards of this life are the real
luminous perfections which are realized in
this world, and which are the cause of eternal life,
for they are the very progress of existence. It is like
the man who passes from the embryonic world to
the state of maturity and becomes the manifestation
of these words: "Blessed, therefore, be God, the
most excellent of Makers."* The rewards of
the other world are peace, the spiritual graces, the
various spiritual gifts in the Kingdom of God,
the gaining of the desires of the heart and the soul,
and the meeting of God in the world of eternity.
In the same way the punishments of the other
world—that is to say, the torments of the other
world—consist in being deprived of the special,
divine blessings and the absolute bounties, and
falling into the lowest degrees of existence. He who

---

*Qur'án 23:14.

is deprived of these divine favors, although he
continues after death, is considered as dead by the
people of truth.   **75**

The Wisdom of the Soul's Journey to God

YOU have asked why it was necessary for the soul
that was from God to make this journey back
to God? . . .

The reality underlying this question is that the
evil spirit, Satan or whatever is interpreted as evil,
refers to the lower nature in man. This baser nature
is symbolized in various ways. In man there are
two expressions: One is the expression of nature;
the other, the expression of the spiritual realm. The
world of nature is defective. Look at it clearly,
casting aside all superstition and imagination. If you
should leave a man uneducated and barbarous in
the wilds of Africa, would there be any doubt about
his remaining ignorant? God has never created an
evil spirit; all such ideas and nomenclature are
symbols expressing the mere human or earthly
nature of man. It is an essential condition of the soil
of earth that thorns, weeds and fruitless trees may
grow from it. Relatively speaking, this is evil; it
is simply the lower state and baser product of
nature.

It is evident, therefore, that man is in need of
divine education and inspiration, that the spirit
and bounties of God are essential to his
development. That is to say, the teachings of Christ
and the Prophets are necessary for his education
and guidance. Why? Because They are the divine

Gardeners Who till the earth of human hearts and
minds. They educate man, uproot the weeds,
burn the thorns and remodel the waste places into
gardens and orchards where fruitful trees grow. The
wisdom and purpose of Their training is that man
must pass from degree to degree of progressive
unfoldment until perfection is attained. For
instance, if a man should live his entire life in one
city, he cannot gain a knowledge of the whole
world. To become perfectly informed he must visit
other cities, see the mountains and valleys, cross the
rivers and traverse the plains. In other words,
without progressive and universal education
perfection will not be attained.

Man must walk in many paths and be
subjected to various processes in his evolution
upward. Physically he is not born in full stature but
passes through consecutive stages of fetus, infant,
childhood, youth, maturity and old age. Suppose he
had the power to remain young throughout his
life. He then would not understand the meaning of
old age and could not believe it existed. If he
could not realize the condition of old age, he would
not know that he was young. He would not know
the difference between young and old without
experiencing the old. Unless you have passed
through the state of infancy, how would you know
this was an infant beside you? If there were no
wrong, how would you recognize the right? If it
were not for sin, how would you appreciate virtue?
If evil deeds were unknown, how could you
commend good actions? If sickness did not exist,
how would you understand health? Evil is
nonexistent; it is the absence of good. Sickness is

the loss of health; poverty, the lack of riches. When
wealth disappears, you are poor; you look within
the treasure box but find nothing there. Without
knowledge there is ignorance; therefore, ignorance
is simply the lack of knowledge. Death is the
absence of life. Therefore, on the one hand we have
existence; on the other, nonexistence, negation or
absence of existence.

Briefly, the journey of the soul is necessary.
The pathway of life is the road which leads to
divine knowledge and attainment. Without training
and guidance the soul could never progress beyond
the conditions of its lower nature, which is ignorant
and defective.   **76**

The Proper Attitude toward Death

A friend asked: "How should one look forward to death?"
'Abdu'l-Bahá answered: "HOW does one look
forward to the goal of any journey? With hope and
with expectation. It is even so with the end of this
earthly journey. In the next world, man will find
himself freed from many of the disabilities
under which he now suffers. Those who have passed
on through death have a sphere of their own. It is
not removed from ours; their work, the work of the
Kingdom, is ours; but it is sanctified from what we
call 'time and place.' Time with us is measured by
the sun. When there is no more sunrise, and no
more sunset, that kind of time does not exist
for man. Those who have ascended have different
attributes from those who are still on earth, yet
there is no real separation."   **77**

The Progress of the Soul after Death

As to the soul of man after death, it remains in the degree of purity to which it has evolved during life in the physical body, and after it is freed from the body, it remains plunged in the ocean of God's mercy.

From the moment the soul leaves the body and arrives in the heavenly world, its evolution is spiritual, and that evolution is: *The approaching unto God.*

In the physical creation, evolution is from one degree of perfection to another. The mineral passes with its mineral perfections to the vegetable; the vegetable, with its perfections, passes to the animal world, and so on to that of humanity. This world is full of seeming contradictions; in each of these kingdoms (mineral, vegetable and animal) life exists in its degree; though when compared to the life in a man, the earth appears to be dead, yet she, too, lives and has a life of her own. In this world things live and die, and live again in other forms of life, but in the world of the spirit it is quite otherwise.

The soul does not evolve from degree to degree as a law—it only evolves nearer to God, by the mercy and bounty of God.   78

Progress in the Next World

Know that nothing which exists remains in a state of repose—that is to say, all things are in motion. Everything is either growing or declining;

all things are either coming from nonexistence
into being, or going from existence into
nonexistence. So this flower, this hyacinth, during a
certain period of time was coming from the world
of nonexistence into being, and now it is going
from being into nonexistence. This state of motion
is said to be essential—that is, natural; it cannot
be separated from beings because it is their essential
requirement, as it is the essential requirement of
fire to burn.

   Thus it is established that this movement is
necessary to existence, which is either growing or
declining. Now, as the spirit continues to exist after
death, it necessarily progresses or declines; and in
the other world to cease to progress is the same
as to decline; but it never leaves its own condition,
in which it continues to develop. For example,
the reality of the spirit of Peter, however far it may
progress will not reach to the condition of the
Reality of Christ; it progresses only in its own
environment.

   Look at this mineral. However far it may
evolve, it only evolves in its own condition; you
cannot bring the crystal to a state where it can
attain to sight. This is impossible. So the moon
which is in the heavens, however far it might
evolve, could never become a luminous sun, but in
its own condition it has apogee and perigee.
However far the disciples might progress, they
could never become Christ. It is true that coal could
become a diamond, but both are in the mineral
condition, and their component elements are the
same.   79

The Progress of the Spirit

ABSOLUTE repose does not exist in nature. All things either make progress or lose ground. Everything moves forward or backward; nothing is without motion. From his birth, a man progresses physically until he reaches maturity; then, having arrived at the prime of his life, he begins to decline, the strength and powers of his body decrease, and he gradually arrives at the hour of death. Likewise, a plant progresses from the seed to maturity; then its life begins to lessen until it fades and dies. A bird soars to a certain height and, having reached the highest possible point in its flight, begins its descent to earth.

Thus it is evident that movement is essential to all existence. All material things progress to a certain point, then begin to decline. This is the law which governs the whole physical creation.

Now let us consider the soul. We have seen that movement is essential to existence; nothing that has life is without motion. All creation, whether of the mineral, vegetable or animal kingdom, is compelled to obey the law of motion; it must either ascend or descend. But with the human soul, there is no decline. Its only movement is towards perfection; growth and progress alone constitute the motion of the soul.

Divine perfection is infinite; therefore, the progress of the soul is also infinite. From the very birth of a human being the soul progresses, the intellect grows and knowledge increases. When the body dies, the soul lives on. All the differing

degrees of created physical beings are limited, but
the soul is limitless!

. . . .

In the world of spirit there is no retrogression.
The world of mortality is a world of contradictions,
of opposites; motion being compulsory, everything
must either go forward or retreat. In the realm of
spirit there is no retreat possible; all movement
is bound to be towards a perfect state. "Progress" is
the expression of spirit in the world of matter.
The intelligence of man, his reasoning powers, his
knowledge, his scientific achievements, all these
being manifestations of the spirit, partake of
the inevitable law of spiritual progress and are,
therefore, of necessity, immortal.

My hope for you is that you will progress in
the world of spirit, as well as in the world of matter,
that your intelligence will develop, your knowledge
will augment, and your understanding be widened.

80

The Means of Progress of the Soul

*Question.—Through what means will the spirit of
man—that is to say, the rational soul—after departing
from this mortal world, make progress?*

Answer.—THE progress of man's spirit in the
divine world, after the severance of its connection
with the body of dust, is through the bounty
and grace of the Lord alone, or through the
intercession and the sincere prayers of other human
souls, or through the charities and important
good works which are performed in its name.   81

Intercession in the Next World

THE wealth of the other world is nearness to God. Consequently, it is certain that those who are near the Divine Court are allowed to intercede, and this intercession is approved by God. But intercession in the other world is not like intercession in this world. It is another thing, another reality, which cannot be expressed in words.

If a wealthy man at the time of his death bequeaths a gift to the poor and miserable, and gives a part of his wealth to be spent for them, perhaps this action may be the cause of his pardon and forgiveness, and of his progress in the divine Kingdom.

Also a father and mother endure the greatest troubles and hardships for their children; and often when the children have reached the age of maturity, the parents pass on to the other world. Rarely does it happen that a father and mother in this world see the reward of the care and trouble they have undergone for their children. Therefore, children, in return for this care and trouble, must show forth charity and beneficence, and must implore pardon and forgiveness for their parents. So you ought, in return for the love and kindness shown you by your father, to give to the poor for his sake, with greatest submission and humility implore pardon and remission of sins, and ask for the supreme mercy.

It is even possible that the condition of those

who have died in sin and unbelief may become
changed—that is to say, they may become the object
of pardon through the bounty of God, not through
His justice—for bounty is giving without desert,
and justice is giving what is deserved. As we
have power to pray for these souls here, so likewise
we shall possess the same power in the other
world, which is the Kingdom of God. Are not all
the people in that world the creatures of God?
Therefore, in that world also they can make
progress. As here they can receive light by their
supplications, there also they can plead for
forgiveness and receive light through entreaties and
supplications. Thus as souls in this world, through
the help of the supplications, the entreaties and
the prayers of the holy ones, can acquire
development, so is it the same after death. Through
their own prayers and supplications they can also
progress, more especially when they are the object
of the intercession of the Holy Manifestations. 82

Soaring in the Kingdom in This World

THOSE souls that, in this day, enter the divine
Kingdom and attain everlasting life, although
materially dwelling on earth, yet in reality soar
in the realm of heaven. Their bodies may linger on
earth, but their spirits travel in the immensity of
space. For as thoughts widen and become illumined,
they acquire the power of flight and transport man
to the Kingdom of God. 83

Greater Perception in the World to Come

CONSIDER how a being, in the world of the womb, was deaf of ear and blind of eye, and mute of tongue; how he was bereft of any perceptions at all. But once, out of that world of darkness, he passed into this world of light; then his eye saw, his ear heard, his tongue spoke. In the same way, once he hath hastened away from this mortal place into the Kingdom of God, then he will be born in the spirit; then the eye of his perception will open, the ear of his soul will hearken, and all the truths of which he was ignorant before will be made plain and clear.

An observant traveler passing along a way will certainly recall his discoveries to mind, unless some accident befall him and efface the memory.

84

The Discovery of Hidden Mysteries

As to thy question regarding discoveries made by the soul after it hath put off its human form: Certainly, that world is a world of perceptions and discoveries, for the interposed veil will be lifted away and the human spirit will gaze upon souls that are above, below, and on a par with itself. It is similar to the condition of a human being in the womb, where his eyes are veiled, and all things are hidden away from him. Once he is born out of the uterine world and entereth this life, he findeth it, with relation to that of the womb, to be a place of perceptions and discoveries. and he

observeth all things through his outer eye. In the
same way, once he hath departed this life, he
will behold, in that world, whatsoever was hidden
from him here: But there he will look upon and
comprehend all things with his inner eye.
There will he gaze on his fellows and his peers, and
those in the ranks above him, and those below.   **85**

The Promise of Recognizing Souls in the Next Life

As to the question whether the souls will
recognize each other in the spiritual world:
This fact is certain; for the Kingdom is the world of
vision where all the concealed realities will
become disclosed. How much more the well-known
souls will become manifest. The mysteries of
which man is heedless in the earthly world, those
will he discover in the heavenly world, and there
will he be informed of the secrets of the truth; how
much more will he recognize or discover persons
with whom he has been associated. Undoubtedly,
the holy souls who find a pure eye and are
favored with insight will, in the kingdom of lights,
be acquainted with all mysteries, and will seek the
bounty of witnessing the reality of every great soul.
They will even manifestly behold the beauty of
God in that world. Likewise, will they find all the
friends of God, both those of the former and recent
times, present in the heavenly assemblage.

The difference and distinction between men
will naturally become realized after their departure
from this mortal world. But this distinction is not
in respect to place, but in respect to the soul and

conscience. For the Kingdom of God is sanctified
(or free) from time and place; it is another
world and another universe. And know thou for a
certainty that in the divine worlds the spiritual
beloved ones will recognize one another, and will
seek union with each other, but a spiritual
union. Likewise, a love that one may have
entertained for anyone will not be forgotten in the
world of the Kingdom, nor wilt thou forget
there the life that thou hadst in the material world.

86

The Relationship between the Living and the Dead

The Mingling of the Departed and the Living

THOSE who have ascended have different attributes from those who are still on earth, yet there is no real separation.

"In prayer there is a mingling of station, a mingling of condition. Pray for them as they pray for you!"   87

The Aid of the Departed for the Living

Someone present asked how it was that in prayer and meditation the heart often turns with instinctive appeal to some friend who has passed into the next life.

'Abdu'l-Bahá answered: "IT is a law of God's creation that the weak should lean upon the strong. Those to whom you turn may be the mediators of God's power to you, even as when on earth. But it is the One Holy Spirit that strengthens all men."   88

Teaching the Departed

Asked whether it was possible through faith and love to bring the new revelation to the knowledge of those who have departed from this life without hearing of it,

'Abdu'l-Bahá replied:—YES, surely! since sincere prayer always has its effect, and it has a great influence in the other world. We are never cut off from those who are there. The real and genuine influence is not in this world but in that other." **89**

Conversation with the Departed

"Can a departed soul converse with someone still on earth?"

'Abdu'l-Bahá.—"A conversation can be held, but not as our conversation. There is no doubt that the forces of the higher worlds interplay with the forces of this plane. The heart of man is open to inspiration; this is spiritual communication. As in a dream one talks with a friend while the mouth is silent, so is it in the conversation of the spirit. A man may converse with the ego within him saying: 'May I do this? Would it be advisable for me to do this work?' Such as this is conversation with the higher self." **90**

The Inefficacy of Mediums and Trances

OUTSIDE the bounty of the Holy Spirit, whatsoever thou hearest as to the effect of trances, or the mediums' trumpets, conveying the singing voices of the dead, is imagination pure and simple. As to the bounty of the Holy Spirit, however, relate whatsoever thou wilt—it cannot be overstated; believe, therefore, whatsoever thou hearest of this. But the persons referred to, the trumpet-people, are entirely shut out from this bounty and receive no portion thereof; their way is an illusion. **91**

The Danger of Tampering with Psychic Forces

To tamper with psychic forces while in this world interferes with the condition of the soul in the world to come. These forces are real, but, normally, are not active on this plane. The child in the womb has its eyes, ears, hands, feet, etc., but they are not in activity. The whole purpose of life in the material world is the coming forth into the world of reality, where those forces will become active. They belong to that world.   92

On the Death of Infants

Question.—What is the condition of children who die before attaining the age of discretion or before the appointed time of birth?

Answer.—THESE infants are under the shadow of the favor of God; and as they have not committed any sin and are not soiled with the impurities of the world of nature, they are the centers of the manifestation of bounty, and the Eye of Compassion will be turned upon them.   93

On the Death of a Child

ALTHOUGH the loss of a son is indeed heartbreaking and beyond the limits of human endurance, yet one who knoweth and understandeth is assured that the son hath not been lost but, rather, hath stepped from this world into another, and she will find him in the divine realm. That reunion shall be for eternity, while in this world separation is inevitable and bringeth with it a burning grief.

Praise be unto God that thou hast faith, art turning thy face toward the everlasting Kingdom and believest in the existence of a heavenly world. Therefore, be thou not disconsolate, do not languish, do not sigh, neither wail nor weep; for agitation and mourning deeply affect his soul in the divine realm.

That beloved child addresseth thee from the hidden world: "O thou kind Mother, thank divine Providence that I have been freed from a small and gloomy cage and, like the birds of the meadows, have soared to the divine world—a world which is spacious, illumined, and ever gay and jubilant. Therefore, lament not, O Mother, and be not grieved; I am not of the lost, nor have I been obliterated and destroyed. I have shaken off the mortal form and have raised my banner in this spiritual world. Following this separation is everlasting companionship. Thou shalt find me in the heaven of the Lord, immersed in an ocean of light." 94

On the Death of a Youth

THE death of that beloved youth and his separation from you have caused the utmost sorrow and grief; for he winged his flight in the flower of his age and the bloom of his youth to the heavenly nest. But he hath been freed from this sorrow-stricken shelter and hath turned his face toward the everlasting nest of the Kingdom, and, being delivered from a dark and narrow world, hath hastened to the sanctified realm of light; therein lieth the consolation of our hearts.

The inscrutable divine wisdom underlieth such heartrending occurrences. It is as if a kind gardener transferreth a fresh and tender shrub from a confined place to a wide open area. This transfer is not the cause of the withering, the lessening or the destruction of that shrub; nay, on the contrary, it maketh it to grow and thrive, acquire freshness and delicacy, become green and bear fruit. This hidden secret is well known to the gardener, but those souls who are unaware of this bounty suppose that the gardener, in his anger and wrath, hath uprooted the shrub. Yet to those who are aware, this concealed fact is manifest, and this predestined decree is considered a bounty. Do not feel grieved or disconsolate, therefore, at the ascension of that bird of faithfulness; nay, under all circumstances pray for that youth, supplicating for him forgiveness and the elevation of his station.

I hope that ye will attain the utmost patience, composure and resignation, and I entreat and implore at the Threshold of Oneness, begging for forgiveness and pardon. My hope from the infinite bounties of God is that He may shelter this dove of the garden of faith, and cause him to abide on the branch of the Supreme Concourse, that he may sing in the best of melodies the praise and glorification of the Lord of Names and Attributes.

95

On the Death of a Partner

BE not grieved at the death of thy respected husband. He hath, verily, attained the meeting of His Lord at the seat of Truth in the presence of the potent King. Do not suppose that thou hast lost him. The veil shall be lifted, and thou shalt behold his face illumined in the Supreme Concourse. Just as God, the Exalted, hath said, "Him will we surely quicken to a happy life." Supreme importance should be attached, therefore, not to this first creation but rather to the future life.

96

THOU hast written of the severe calamity that hath befallen thee—the death of thy respected husband. That honorable man hath been so subjected to the stress and strain of this world that his greatest wish was for deliverance from it. Such is this mortal abode: a storehouse of afflictions and suffering. It is ignorance that binds man to it, for no comfort can be secured by any soul in this world, from monarch down to the most humble commoner. If once this life should offer a man a sweet cup, a hundred bitter ones will follow; such is the condition of this world. The wise man, therefore, doth not attach himself to this mortal life and doth not depend upon it; at some moments, even, he eagerly wisheth for death that he may thereby be freed from these sorrows and afflictions. Thus it is seen that some, under extreme pressure of anguish, have committed suicide.

As to thy husband, rest assured. He will be

immersed in the ocean of pardon and forgiveness
and will become the recipient of bounty and favor.
Strive thine utmost to give his child a Bahá'í
training so that when he attaineth maturity he may
be merciful, illumined and heavenly. 97

On the Death of the Handicapped

As to those souls who are born into this life as
ethereal and radiant entities and yet, on
account of their handicaps and trials, are deprived of
great and real advantages, and leave the world
without having lived to the full—certainly this is a
cause for grieving. This is the reason why the
universal Manifestations of God unveil Their
countenances to man, and endure every calamity
and sore affliction, and lay down Their lives as
a ransom; it is to make these very people, the ready
ones, the ones who have capacity, to become
dawning points of light, and to bestow upon them
the life that fadeth never. This is the true sacrifice:
the offering of oneself, even as did Christ, as a
ransom for the life of the world. 98

On Those Who Die in Calamities

. . . When I consider this calamity* in another
aspect, I am consoled by the realization that the
worlds of God are infinite; that though they were
deprived of this existence, they have other
opportunities in the life beyond, even as Christ has

---

*The sinking of the *Titanic,* 1912.

said, "In my Father's house are many mansions."
They were called away from the temporary and
transferred to the eternal; they abandoned this
material existence and entered the portals of the
spiritual world. Foregoing the pleasures and
comforts of the earthly, they now partake of a joy
and happiness far more abiding and real, for
they have hastened to the Kingdom of God. The
mercy of God is infinite, and it is our duty to
remember these departed souls in our prayers and
supplications that they may draw nearer and nearer
to the Source itself.

These human conditions may be likened to the
matrix of the mother from which a child is to be
born into the spacious outer world. At first the
infant finds it very difficult to reconcile itself to its
new existence. It cries as if not wishing to be
separated from its narrow abode and imagining that
life is restricted to that limited space. It is reluctant
to leave its home, but nature forces it into this
world. Having come into its new conditions, it finds
that it has passed from darkness into a sphere of
radiance; from gloomy and restricted surroundings
it has been transferred to a spacious and delightful
environment. Its nourishment was the blood of the
mother; now it finds delicious food to enjoy. Its new
life is filled with brightness and beauty; it looks
with wonder and delight upon the mountains,
meadows and fields of green, the rivers and
fountains, the wonderful stars; it breathes the life-
quickening atmosphere; and then it praises God for
its release from the confinement of its former
condition and attainment to the freedom of a new
realm. This analogy expresses the relation of the

temporal world to the life hereafter—the transition
of the soul of man from darkness and uncertainty
to the light and reality of the eternal Kingdom. At
first it is very difficult to welcome death, but after
attaining its new condition the soul is grateful, for it
has been released from the bondage of the limited
to enjoy the liberties of the unlimited. It has
been freed from a world of sorrow, grief and trials
to live in a world of unending bliss and joy. The
phenomenal and physical have been abandoned in
order that it may attain the opportunities of the
ideal and spiritual. Therefore, the souls of
those who have passed away from earth and
completed their span of mortal pilgrimage in the
Titanic disaster have hastened to a world superior to
this. They have soared away from these conditions
of darkness and dim vision into the realm of
light. These are the only considerations which can
comfort and console those whom they have left
behind.   99

Reincarnation

THOU didst write of reincarnation. A belief in
reincarnation goeth far back into the ancient
history of almost all peoples, and was held even by
the philosophers of Greece, the Roman sages, the
ancient Egyptians, and the great Assyrians.
Nevertheless, such superstitions and sayings are but
absurdities in the sight of God.

The major argument of the reincarnationists
was this, that according to the justice of God, each
must receive his due: Whenever a man is afflicted
with some calamity, for example, this is because of

some wrong he hath committed. But take a child that is still in its mother's womb, the embryo but newly formed, and that child is blind, deaf, lame, defective—what sin hath such a child committed, to deserve its afflictions? They answer that, although to outward seeming the child, still in the womb, is guilty of no sin—nevertheless he perpetrated some wrong when in his previous form, and thus he came to deserve his punishment.

These individuals, however, have overlooked the following point. If creation went forward according to only one rule, how could the all-encompassing Power make Itself felt? How could the Almighty be the One Who "doeth as He pleaseth and ordaineth as He willeth"?*

Briefly, a return is indeed referred to in the Holy Scriptures, but by this is meant the return of the qualities, conditions, effects, perfections, and inner realities of the lights which recur in every dispensation. The reference is not to specific, individual souls and identities.

It may be said, for instance, that this lamplight is last night's come back again, or that last year's rose hath returned to the garden this year. Here the reference is not to the individual reality, the fixed identity, the specialized being of that other rose; rather doth it mean that the qualities, the distinctive characteristics of that other light, that other flower, are present now, in these. Those perfections, that is, those graces and gifts of a former springtime, are back again this year. We say, for example, that this

---

*Cf. Qur'án 3:35; 2:254.

fruit is the same as last year's; but we are thinking
only of the delicacy, bloom and freshness, and
the sweet taste of it; for it is obvious that that
impregnable center of reality, that specific identity,
can never return.

What peace, what ease and comfort did the
Holy Ones of God ever discover during Their
sojourn in this nether world, that They should
continually seek to come back and live this
life again? Doth not a single turn at this anguish,
these afflictions, these calamities, these body blows,
these dire straits, suffice, that They should wish
for repeated visits to the life of this world? This cup
was not so sweet that one would care to drink of it
a second time.

Therefore, do the lovers of the Abhá Beauty
wish for no other recompense but to reach that
station where they may gaze upon Him in the
Realm of Glory, and they walk no other path save
over desert sands of longing for those exalted
heights. They seek that ease and solace which will
abide forever, and those bestowals that are sanctified
beyond the understanding of the worldly mind.

100

The Imperishable Gift

Attraction to the Kingdom

O THOU who art attracted to the Kingdom of God! Every soul seeketh an object and cherisheth a desire, and day and night striveth to attain his aim. One craveth riches, another thirsteth for glory and still another yearneth for fame, for art, for prosperity and the like. Yet finally all are doomed to loss and disappointment. One and all they leave behind them all that is theirs and empty-handed hasten to the realm beyond, and all their labors shall be in vain. To dust they shall all return, denuded, depressed, disheartened and in utter despair.

But, praised be the Lord, thou art engaged in that which secureth for thee a gain that shall eternally endure; and that is naught but thine attraction to the Kingdom of God, thy faith, and thy knowledge, the enlightenment of thine heart, and thine earnest endeavor to promote the divine teachings.

Verily, this gift is imperishable and this wealth is a treasure from on high! 101

The Eternal Kingdom of God

T HIS phenomenal world will not remain in an unchanging condition even for a short while. Second after second it undergoes change and transformation. Every foundation will finally become collapsed; every glory and splendor will at last vanish and disappear, but the Kingdom of God is eternal and the heavenly sovereignty and majesty will stand firm, everlasting. Hence in the estimation of a wise man the mat in the Kingdom of God is preferable to the throne of the government of the world. 102

The Beauty That Lasts

MORTAL charm shall fade away, roses give way to thorns, and beauty and youth shall live their day and be no more. But that which eternally endureth is the Beauty of the True One, for its splendor perisheth not and its glory lasteth forever; its charm is all-powerful and its attraction infinite. Well is it then with that countenance that reflecteth the splendor of the Light of the Beloved One! The Lord be praised, thou hast been illumined with this Light, hast acquired the pearl of true knowledge, and hast spoken the Word of Truth. 103

The True Kingdom

GRIEVE thou not over the troubles and hardships of this nether world, nor be thou glad in times of ease and comfort, for both shall pass away. This present life is even as a swelling wave, or a mirage, or drifting shadows. Could ever a distorted image on the desert serve as refreshing waters? No, by the Lord of Lords! Never can reality and the mere semblance of reality be one, and wide is the

difference between fancy and fact, between truth
and the phantom thereof.

Know thou that the Kingdom is the real
world, and this nether place is only its shadow
stretching out. A shadow hath no life of its own; its
existence is only a fantasy, and nothing more; it is
but images reflected in water, and seeming as
pictures to the eye.   **104**

The Kingdom of Your Lord

O YE loved ones of God! Know ye that the world
is even as a mirage rising over the sands,
that the thirsty mistaketh for water. The wine of
this world is but a vapor in the desert, its pity and
compassion but toil and trouble, the repose it
proffereth only weariness and sorrow. Abandon it to
those who belong to it, and turn your faces unto
the Kingdom of your Lord, the All-Merciful, that
His grace and bounty may cast their dawning
splendors over you, and a heavenly table may be sent
down for you, and your Lord may bless you, and
shower His riches upon you to gladden your bosoms
and fill your hearts with bliss, to attract your
minds, and cleanse your souls, and console your
eyes.   **105**

The Life That Will Not Die

THESE few brief days shall pass away, this present
life shall vanish from our sight; the roses of
this world shall be fresh and fair no more, the
garden of this earth's triumphs and delights shall

droop and fade. The spring season of life shall turn into the autumn of death, the bright joy of palace halls give way to moonless dark within the tomb. And therefore is none of this worth loving at all, and to this the wise will not anchor his heart.

He who hath knowledge and power will, rather, seek out the glory of heaven, and spiritual distinction, and the life that dieth not. And such a one longeth to approach the sacred Threshold of God; for in the tavern of this swiftly passing world the man of God will not lie drunken, nor will he even for a moment take his ease, nor stain himself with any fondness for this earthly life.   **106**

Gems for Meditation

Selections from the Hidden Words

O SON OF MAN!

THOU art My dominion and My dominion
perisheth not; wherefore fearest thou
thy perishing? Thou art My light and My light
shall never be extinguished; why dost thou dread
extinction? Thou are My glory and My glory fadeth
not; thou art My robe and My robe shall never be
outworn. Abide then in thy love for Me, that
thou mayest find Me in the realm of glory.   107

O SON OF THE SUPREME!

I HAVE made death a messenger of joy to thee.
Wherefore dost thou grieve? I made the light to
shed on thee its splendor. Why dost thou veil
thyself therefrom?   108

O SON OF MAN!

ASCEND unto My heaven, that thou mayest obtain
the joy of reunion, and from the chalice of
imperishable glory quaff the peerless wine.   109

O MY SERVANT!

ABANDON not for that which perisheth an
everlasting dominion, and cast not away
celestial sovereignty for a worldy desire. This is the
river of everlasting life that hath flowed from the
wellspring of the pen of the merciful; well is it with
them that drink!   110

O MY SERVANT!

FREE thyself from the fetters of this world, and loose thy soul from the prison of self. Seize thy chance, for it will come to thee no more.   **111**

O SON OF MY HANDMAID!

DIDST thou behold immortal sovereignty, thou wouldst strive to pass from this fleeting world. But to conceal the one from thee and to reveal the other is a mystery which none but the pure in heart can comprehend.   **112**

O COMPANION OF MY THRONE!

. . . LIVE then the days of thy life, that are less than a fleeting moment, with thy mind stainless, thy heart unsullied, thy thoughts pure, and thy nature sanctified, so that, free and content, thou mayest put away this mortal frame, and repair unto the mystic paradise and abide in the eternal kingdom for evermore.   **113**

O SON OF WORLDLINESS!

PLEASANT is the realm of being, wert thou to attain thereto; glorious is the domain of eternity, shouldst thou pass beyond the world of mortality; sweet is the holy ecstasy if thou drinkest of the mystic chalice from the hands of the celestial Youth. Shouldst thou attain this station, thou wouldst be freed from destruction and death, from toil and sin.   **114**

O CHILDREN OF NEGLIGENCE!

SET not your affections on mortal sovereignty and rejoice not therein. Ye are even as the unwary bird that with full confidence warbleth upon the bough; till of a sudden the fowler Death throws it upon the dust, and the melody, the form and the color are gone, leaving not a trace. Wherefore take heed, O bondslaves of desire! **115**

O SON OF BEING!

THY Paradise is My love; thy heavenly home reunion with Me. Enter therein and tarry not. This is that which hath been destined for thee in Our kingdom above and Our exalted dominion.

116

O SON OF THE SUPREME!

TO the eternal I call thee, yet thou dost seek that which perisheth. What hath made thee turn away from Our desire and seek thine own? **117**

O SON OF SPIRIT!

WITH the joyful tidings of light I hail thee: rejoice! To the court of holiness I summon thee; abide therein that thou mayest live in peace for evermore. **118**

O SON OF MAN!

THE light hath shone on thee from the horizon of the sacred Mount and the spirit of enlightenment hath breathed in the Sinai of thy

heart. Wherefore, free thyself from the veils of idle
fancies and enter into My court, that thou mayest
be fit for everlasting life and worthy to meet
Me. Thus may death not come upon thee, neither
weariness nor trouble.   **119**

O OFFSPRING OF DUST!

BE not content with the ease of a passing day, and
deprive not thyself of everlasting rest. Barter
not the garden of eternal delight for the dust-heap
of a mortal world. Up from thy prison ascend
unto the glorious meads above, and from thy mortal
cage wing thy flight unto the paradise of the
Placeless.   **120**

Prayers for the Departed

(The Prayer for the Dead is to be used for Bahá'ís over the age of fifteen. "It is the only Bahá'í obligatory prayer which is to be recited in congregation; it is to be recited by one believer while all present stand. There is no requirement to face the Qiblih when reciting this prayer."—*A Synopsis and Codification of the Kitáb-i-Aqdas*)

O MY God! This is Thy servant and the son of Thy servant who hath believed in Thee and in Thy signs, and set his face towards Thee, wholly detached from all except Thee. Thou art, verily, of those who show mercy the most merciful.

Deal with him, O Thou Who forgivest the sins of men and concealest their faults, as beseemeth the heaven of Thy bounty and the ocean of Thy grace. Grant him admission within the precincts of Thy transcendent mercy that was before the foundation of earth and heaven. There is no God but Thee, the Ever-Forgiving, the Most Generous.

Let him, then, repeat six times the greeting "Alláh-u-Abhá," and then repeat nineteen times each of the following verses:

> We all, verily, worship God.
> We all, verily, bow down before God.
> We all, verily, are devoted unto God.
> We all, verily, give praise unto God.
> We all, verily, yield thanks unto God.
> We all, verily, are patient in God.

(If the dead be a woman, let him say:
This is Thy handmaiden and the daughter of Thy handmaiden, etc. . . .) —*Bahá'u'lláh*
121

GLORY be to Thee, O Lord my God! Abase not
him whom Thou has exalted through the
power of Thine everlasting sovereignty, and remove
not far from Thee him whom Thou hast caused to
enter the tabernacle of Thine eternity. Wilt
Thou cast away, O my God, him whom Thou hast
overshadowed with Thy Lordship, and wilt Thou
turn away from Thee, O my Desire, him to whom
Thou hast been a refuge? Canst Thou degrade
him whom Thou hast uplifted, or forget him
whom Thou didst enable to remember Thee?

Glorified, immensely glorified art Thou! Thou
art He Who from everlasting hath been the King
of the entire creation and its Prime Mover, and
Thou wilt to everlasting remain the Lord of
all created things and their Ordainer. Glorified art
Thou, O my God! If Thou ceasest to be merciful
unto Thy servants, who, then, will show mercy
unto them; and if Thou refusest to succor Thy
loved ones, who is there that can succor them?

Glorified, immeasurably glorified art Thou!
Thou art adored in Thy truth, and Thee do we all,
verily, worship; and Thou art manifest in Thy
justice, and to Thee do we all, verily, bear witness.
Thou art, in truth, beloved in Thy grace. No God is
there but Thee, the Help in Peril, the Self-
Subsisting.   —*Bahá'u'lláh*

122

HE is God, exalted is He, the Lord of loving-
kindness and bounty!

Glory be unto Thee, Thou, O my God, the
Lord Omnipotent. I testify to Thine omnipotence

and Thy might, thy sovereignty and Thy loving-kindness, Thy grace and Thy power, the oneness of Thy Being and the unity of Thine Essence, Thy sanctity and exaltation above the world of being and all that is therein.

O my God! Thou seest me detached from all save Thee, holding fast unto Thee and turning unto the ocean of Thy bounty, to the heaven of Thy favor, to the Daystar of Thy grace.

Lord! I bear witness that in Thy servant Thou hast reposed Thy Trust, and that is the Spirit wherewith Thou hast given life to the world.

I ask of Thee, by the splendor of the Orb of Thy Revelation, mercifully to accept from him that which he hath achieved in Thy days. Grant then that he may be invested with the glory of Thy good-pleasure and adorned with Thine acceptance.

O my Lord! I myself and all created things bear witness unto Thy might, and I pray Thee not to turn away from Thyself this spirit that hath ascended unto thee, unto Thy heavenly place, Thine exalted Paradise and Thy retreats of nearness, O Thou who art the Lord of all men!

Grant, then, O my God, that Thy servant may consort with Thy chosen ones, Thy saints and Thy Messengers in heavenly places that the pen cannot tell nor the tongue recount.

O My Lord, the poor one hath verily hastened unto the Kingdom of Thy wealth, the stranger unto his home within Thy precincts, he that is sore athirst to the heavenly river of Thy bounty. Deprive him not, O Lord, from his share of the banquet of Thy grace and from the favor of

Thy bounty. Thou art in truth the Almighty, the Gracious, the All-Bountiful.

O my God, Thy Trust hath been returned unto Thee. It behooveth Thy grace and Thy bounty that have compassed Thy dominions on earth and in heaven, to vouchsafe unto Thy newly welcomed one Thy gifts and Thy bestowals, and the fruits of the tree of Thy grace! Powerful art Thou to do as Thou willest; there is none other God but Thee, the Gracious, the Most Bountiful, the Compassionate, the Bestower, the Pardoner, the Precious, the All-Knowing.

I testify, O my Lord, that Thou hast enjoined upon men to honor their guest, and he that hath ascended unto Thee hath verily reached Thee and attained Thy Presence. Deal with him then according to Thy grace and bounty! By Thy glory, I know of a certainty that Thou wilt not withhold Thyself from that which Thou hast commanded Thy servants, nor wilt Thou deprive him that hath clung to the cord of Thy bounty and hath ascended to the Dayspring of Thy wealth.

There is none other God but Thee, the One, the Single, the Powerful, the Omniscient, the Bountiful. —*Bahá'u'lláh*

123

LAUDED art Thou, O my God: My trespasses have waxed mighty and my sins have assumed grievous proportions. How disgraceful my plight will prove to be in Thy holy presence. I have failed to know Thee to the extent Thou didst reveal Thyself unto me; I have failed to worship Thee with a devotion worthy of Thy summons; I have

failed to obey Thee through not treading the path
of Thy love in the manner Thou didst inspire me.

Thy might beareth me witness, O my God:
What befitteth Thee is far greater and more exalted
than any being could attempt to accomplish.
Indeed, nothing can ever comprehend Thee as is
worthy of Thee, nor can any servile creature
worship Thee as beseemeth Thine adoration. So
perfect and comprehensive is Thy proof, O my
God, that its inner essence transcendeth the
description of any soul, and so abundant are the
outpourings of Thy gifts that no faculty can
appraise their infinite range.

O my God! O my Master! I beseech Thee by
Thy manifold bounties and by the pillars which
sustain Thy throne of glory, to have pity on these
lowly people who are powerless to bear the
unpleasant things of this fleeting life, how much
less then can they bear Thy chastisement in the life
to come—a chastisement which is ordained by
Thy justice, called forth by Thy wrath and
will continue to exist forever.

I beg Thee by Thyself, O my God, my Lord
and my Master, to intercede in my behalf. I have
fled from Thy justice unto Thy mercy. For my
refuge I am seeking Thee and such as turn not away
from Thy path, even for a twinkling of an eye—
they for whose sake Thou didst create the creation
as a token of Thy grace and bounty.   —*The Báb*

124

DO thou ordain for me, O Lord, every good
thing Thou hast created or wilt create, and
shield me from whatever evil Thou abhorrest from

among the things Thou hast caused or wilt cause to
exist. In truth, Thy knowledge embraceth all
things. Praised be Thou, verily, no God is there but
Thee, and nothing whatsoever in the heavens or
on the earth and all that is between them can ever
thwart Thy purpose. Indeed potent art Thou
over all things.

Far be it from the sublimity of Thy Being, O
my God, that anyone seek Thy loving-kindness
or favor. Far be it from Thy transcendent glory that
anyone entreat Thee for the evidences of Thy
bestowals and tender mercy. Too high art Thou for
any soul to beseech the revelation of Thy gracious
providence and loving care, and too sanctified is
Thy glory for anyone to beg of Thee the
outpourings of Thy blessings and of Thy heavenly
bounty and grace. Throughout Thy kingdom of
heaven and earth, which is endowed with manifold
bounties, Thou art immeasurably glorified above
aught whereunto any identity could be ascribed.

All that I beg of Thee, O my God, is to enable
me, ere my soul departeth from my body, to attain
Thy good-pleasure, even were it granted to me for a
moment tinier than the infinitesimal fraction of a
mustard seed. For if it departeth while Thou art
pleased with me, then I shall be free from
every concern or anxiety; but if it abandoneth me
while Thou art displeased with me, then, even had
I wrought every good deed, none would be of any
avail, and had I earned every honor and glory, none
would serve to exalt me.

I earnestly beseech Thee then, O my God, to
graciously bestow Thy good-pleasure upon me

when Thou dost cause me to ascend unto Thee and
make me appear before Thy holy presence,
inasmuch as Thou hast, from everlasting, been the
God of immense bounty unto the people of Thy
realm, and the Lord of most excellent gifts to
all that dwell in the exalted heaven of Thine
omnipotence.   —*The Báb*

125

I BEG Thy forgiveness, O my God, and implore
pardon after the manner Thou wishest Thy
servants to direct themselves to Thee. I beg of Thee
to wash away our sins as befitteth Thy Lordship,
and to forgive me, my parents, and those who
in Thy estimation have entered the abode of Thy
love in a manner which is worthy of Thy
transcendent sovereignty and well beseemeth the
glory of Thy celestial power.

O my God! Thou hast inspired my soul to
offer its supplication to Thee, and but for Thee, I
would not call upon Thee. Lauded and glorified art
Thou; I yield Thee praise inasmuch as Thou didst
reveal Thyself unto me, and I beg Thee to
forgive me, since I have fallen short in my duty to
know Thee and have failed to walk in the path
of Thy love.   —*The Báb*

126

GLORY be unto Thee, O God. How can I make
mention of Thee while Thou art sanctified
from the praise of all mankind. Magnified be Thy
Name, O God. Thou art the King, the Eternal
Truth; Thou knowest what is in the heavens and on

the earth, and unto Thee must all return. Thou
hast sent down Thy divinely ordained Revelation
according to a clear measure. Praised art Thou,
O Lord! At Thy behest Thou dost render victorious
whomsoever Thou willest, through the hosts of
heaven and earth and whatsoever existeth between
them. Thou art the Sovereign, the Eternal Truth,
the Lord of invincible might.

Glorified art Thou, O Lord. Thou forgivest at
all times the sins of such among Thy servants as
implore Thy pardon. Wash away my sins and the
sins of those who seek Thy forgiveness at dawn,
who pray to Thee in the daytime and in the night
season, who yearn after naught save God, who offer
up whatsoever God hath graciously bestowed
upon them, who celebrate Thy praise at morn and
eventide, and who are not remiss in their duties.

—*The Báb*

127

O THOU forgiving Lord!
    Although some souls have spent the days of
their lives in ignorance, and became estranged
and contumacious, yet, with one wave from the
ocean of Thy forgiveness, all those encompassed by
sin will be set free. Whomsoever Thou willest
Thou makest a confidant, and whosoever is not the
object of Thy choice is accounted a transgressor.
Shouldst Thou deal with us with Thy justice, we
are all naught but sinners and deserving to be shut
out from Thee, but shouldst Thou uphold mercy,
every sinner would be made pure and every stranger

a friend. Bestow, then, Thy forgiveness and pardon,
and grant Thy mercy unto all.

Thou art the Forgiver, the Lightgiver and the
Omnipotent.   —'Abdu'l-Bahá

128

O MY God! O Thou forgiver of sins, bestower of
gifts, dispeller of afflictions!

Verily, I beseech Thee to forgive the sins of
such as have abandoned the physical garment and
have ascended to the spiritual world.

O my Lord! Purify them from trespasses,
dispel their sorrows, and change their darkness into
light. Cause them to enter the garden of happiness,
cleanse them with the most pure water, and grant
them to behold Thy splendors on the loftiest
mount.   —'Abdu'l-Bahá

129

O MY God! O my God! Verily, thy servant,
humble before the majesty of Thy divine
supremacy, lowly at the door of Thy oneness, hath
believed in Thee and in Thy verses, hath testified to
Thy word, hath been enkindled with the fire of
Thy love, hath been immersed in the depths of the
ocean of Thy knowledge, hath been attracted by
Thy breezes, hath relied upon Thee, hath turned his
face to Thee, hath offered his supplications to
Thee, and hath been assured of Thy pardon and
forgiveness. He hath abandoned this mortal life and
hath flown to the kingdom of immortality,
yearning for the favor of meeting Thee.

O Lord, glorify his station, shelter him under
the pavilion of Thy supreme mercy, cause him to
enter Thy glorious paradise, and perpetuate his
existence in Thine exalted rose garden, that he may
plunge into the sea of light in the world of
mysteries.

Verily, Thou art the Generous, the Powerful,
the Forgiver and the Bestower.   —'Abdu'l-Bahá

References

References

Abbreviations Used

ABL   *'Abdu'l-Bahá in London: Addresses and Notes of Conversations*, new ed., 1982

BNE   *Bahá'u'lláh and the New Era: An Introduction to the Bahá'í Faith*, 4th rev. ed., 1980

BP   *Bahá'í Prayers: A Selection of Prayers Revealed by Bahá'u'lláh, the Báb, and 'Abdu'l-Bahá*, new ed., 1982

BW   *The Bahá'í World: An International Record, Volume XV, 1968–1973*, 1975

BWF   *Bahá'í World Faith: Selected Writings of Bahá'u'lláh and 'Abdu'l-Bahá*, 1976

ESW   *Epistle to the Son of the Wolf*, rev. ed., 1953

GL   *Gleanings from the Writings of Bahá'u'lláh*, 2d ed., 1976

HWA   *The Hidden Words of Bahá'u'lláh* (Arabic), 1982

HWP   *The Hidden Words of Bahá'u'lláh* (Persian), 1982

KI   *Kitáb-i-Íqán: The Book of Certitude*, 2d ed., 1950

NT   New translation provided by the Universal House of Justice, 1984

PM   *Prayers and Meditations*, 1938

PT   *Paris Talks: Addresses Given by 'Abdu'l-Bahá in Paris in 1911*, 11th ed., 1969

PUP   *The Promulgation of Universal Peace: Talks Delivered by 'Abdu'l-Bahá during His Visit to the United States and Canada in 1912*, 2d ed., 1982

SAQ   *Some Answered Questions*, 5th ed., 1981

SV   *The Seven Valleys and the Four Valleys*, 3d ed., 1978

SWAB   *Selections from the Writings of 'Abdu'l-Bahá*, 1978

SWB   *Selections from the Writings of the Báb*, 1976

TB   *Tablets of Bahá'u'lláh Revealed after the Kitáb-i-Aqdas,*
        1978
TDP   *Tablets of the Divine Plan: Revealed by 'Abdu'l-Bahá to*
        the North American Bahá'ís, rev. ed., 1977

Selections from the Writings of Bahá'u'lláh

1	GL 329	12	GL 164–65	23	GL 236
2	KI 120–21	13	GL 132–33	24	GL 251
3	GL 65	14	GL 140–41	25	GL 247
4	GL 77–78	15	TB 189	26	GL 307–08
5	GL 149	16	KI 118	27	GL 126
6	GL 158–62	17	GL 70–71	28	GL 345–46
7	GL 155–58	18	GL 328–29	29	TB 265–66
8	GL 169–71	19	GL 261	30	GL 138–39
9	GL 153–55	20	ESW 56	31	GL 320–21
10	GL 151–53	21	GL 321–22		
11	SV 32–33	22	TB 267		

Selections from the Writings of The Báb

32	SWB 162	39	SWB 106–07	46	SWB 153
33	SWB 161	40	SWB 88–89	47	SWB 62–63
34	SWB 50	41	SWB 82–83	48	SWB 52
35	SWB 95	42	SWB 77	49	SWB 163
36	SWB 157	43	SWB 79	50	SWB 48
37	SWB 157–58	44	SWB 87		
38	SWB 78	45	SWB 145		

Selections from the Writings of 'Abdu'l-Bahá

51	PT 90–94	60	PT 96–99	69	SWAB 169–70
52	SAQ 225–26	61	SAQ 208–09	70	SAQ 251–53
53	BW, XV, 40	62	BW, XV, 43	71	SAQ 241–43
54	SWAB 184–85	63	BW, XV, 38	72	SWAB 192
55	PT 85	64	PT 65–66	73	SWAB 193–94
56	PT 25	65	PT 17	74	PUP 225–27
57	SAQ 239–40	66	PT 86–87	75	SAQ 223–25
58	SAQ 151–52	67	SAQ 227–29	76	PUP 294–96
59	BWF 367	68	PUP 242–43	77	ABL 95–96

78 PT 66–67   87 ABL 96   97   SWAB 200–01
79 SAQ 233–34   88 ABL 97   98   SWAB 64–65
80 PT 88–90   89 BNE 194   99   PUP 47–48
81 SAQ 240   90 PT 179   100 SWAB 183–84
82 SAQ 231–32   91 SWAB 160–61   101 SWAB 204–05
83 SWAB 202   92 BNE 193   102 TDP 73
84 SWAB 177   93 SAQ 240   103 SWAB 204
85 SWAB 170–71   94 SWAB 201   104 SWAB 177–78
86 BWF 367,   95 SWAB 199–200   105 SWAB 186
    BNE 190   96 SWAB 197   106 SWAB 220–21

Selections from the Hidden Words of Bahá'u'lláh

107 HWA 14   112 HWP 41   117 HWA 23
108 HWA 32   113 HWP 44   118 HWA 33
109 HWA 61   114 HWP 70   119 HWA 63
110 HWA 37   115 HWP 75   120 HWP 39
111 HWP 40   116 HWA 6

Prayers for the Departed

121 PM 260–61   125 SWB 187–88   129 BP 45–46
122 PM 261–62   126 SWB 210   130 BP 46–47
123 BP 43–45   127 SWB 177
124 SWB 203–04   128 NT

Index

Index

Acts. *See* Deeds

Ark, Crimson, 12

Arts, the. *See* Discoveries and inventions

Balance
of Justice, 27
Word of God is, 34

Bible, quotations from the
disciples born of God, 83
man born of water and spirit, 22–23, 82
many mansions in Father's house, 104

Body. *See* Man, body of

Candle, everlasting, 25

Children
death of, 99–101
duties of, toward parents, 92

Christ, 35–36. *See also* Bible, quotations from the
Kingdom of, 49
meets Moses and Elias, 72–73
ransom for life of world, 103

Creation, 4. *See also* Discoveries and inventions; Man; World; Worlds of God
aim of, 46
all living things show signs of existence, 45–46, 49–50
everything is in motion, 88–91
human evolution, 46, 79, 86
kingdoms of, 46, 50, 53–54
each thing has paradise of perfection, 37
souls of lower creatures, 53
species are phenomenal, 55

unaware of each other's existence, 78
of man, 79
man is crowning-point of creation, 57
man is sum of every previous creation, 53, 54
physical, is perishable, 45, 55–56
purpose of
to lead to knowledge of God, 7
true believer is originating, 21

Death, physical, 45. *See also* Life, physical; Life after death
as absence of life, 87
body to be treated with respect, 34
communication with the departed, 98
of handicapped, 103
inevitability of, 33
of infants and children, 99–101
like birth of child from womb, 104–05
one should look forward to, 87
messenger of joy, 115
prayer for departed is important, 97–98, 104
prayers for departed, 121–30
resurrection, 23, 35
of spouse, 102–03
state of soul at time of, depends on God's pleasure, 126
of *Titanic* passengers, 103–05

Death, spiritual, 23, 29, 40, 76–77, 84–85. *See also* Life, spiritu-

Death, spiritual *(continued)*
    al; Life after death; Soul
  true death is, 34
Deeds
  deed is its own reward, 22
  manifested by volition, 5
  philanthropic, 80, 92
  worth of, estimated after death,
    12–13, 27, 33, 42, 52
  recompense for every act, 22
Devil. *See* Satan
Discoveries and inventions, 8, 10,
  69–73, 78
  the arts, 8, 10
Diseases. *See* Illnesses, soul inde-
    pendent of bodily
Dreams, 9, 16–17, 66, 69, 98

Earth. *See* World
Education. *See* Life, spiritual, de-
    velopment of; Soul, devel-
    opment and progress of
Elias, meeting of, with Christ,
    72–73
Eternal life. *See* Life, spiritual; Life
    after death
Evil, 85–86
Evolution, 46, 79, 86
  movement necessary to exist-
    ence, 88–91
Existence
  absolute, 11
  contingent, 11
  movement necessary to, 88–91
Extrasensory perception. *See also*
    Dreams
  communication with departed,
    98
  danger in tampering with
    psychic forces, 99

Fate, 19–20
Fire, 38, 41. *See also* Hell
  of unbelief, 23
Free will, 5

God
  as creator, 4

good-pleasure of, 126
love of, 24
man created by, 4–5
man's knowledge of, 4–5, 7
oneness (unity) of, 39–40
presence of
  attaining, 9, 30
  is presence of Manifestation,
    38
Word of, is Balance, 34

Handicapped, death of, 103
Heaven. *See* Life after death
Hell. *See also* Death, spiritual; Life
    after death; Judgment
  of existence, 82
  fire, 22–23, 38, 41
  remoteness, 23
  of unbelief, 23
Husband, death of, 102–03

Illnesses, soul independent of bod-
    ily, 13–15, 63
Illusion, world is, 24
Imagination, 71
Immortality. *See* Life after death;
    Soul
Infant, death of, 99
Intercession, 91–93
Inventions. *See* Discoveries and in-
    ventions

Jesus. *See* Christ
Judgment, 27–29, 33, 34, 35, 38
  chastisement, 125
  Day of Resurrection, 35–36, 38
  deeds, worth of, estimated
    12–13, 27
  infidels shall bemoan plight, 13
Justice, 125, 128
  Balance of, 27

Kingdom (heaven). *See* Life after
    death
Kingdoms of creation. *See* Crea-
    tion; Worlds of God
Koran, quotation from, 84

Life, physical. *See also* Death, phys-
     ical; Man
  is not true life, 3, 109–10
  transitory worthlessness of
       24–29, 108–11, 116, 117,
       118
     black in eye of dead ant, 25
     storehouse of afflictions, 102
Life, spiritual, 23, 28–30. *See also*
     Death, spiritual
  development of, 57–59, 80–85
     houses floods can never de-
          stroy, 24
     loose soul from prison of self,
          116
     man ignores, 81–82
     steps to achieving perfections,
          80–81
  divine spirit unveils mysteries,
       70
  divine tree with good fruit, 58
  eternal life can be attained while
       on earth, 93
  love of God, 24–26
  meaning of, 75–77, 82–85
  realm of being, 116
  rewards of, 82–85
  true life is not life of flesh, 3,
       108–11
  visions, 71–73
Life after death, 37–42, 74–77,
     103–05. *See also* Deeds;
     Judgment; Soul; Worlds of
     God
  attaining presence of God, 9–10,
       30
  children and, 99–101
  eternal life
     can be attained while on
          earth, 93
     Kingdom of God is eternal,
          109
     meaning of, 74–77, 82–85
  existence of
     denial of, 78–79
     proof of, 50–52, 75–76
  heaven, 74–77
     Maids of, 10

hell fire, 22–23, 38, 41
the Kingdom, 74–77
  can attain, while still on
       earth, 93
  has no place but is connected
       with man, 76
  is eternal, 109
  is hidden but plain as day,
       77
  mat in, preferable to throne,
       109
like life of child after womb,
     104–05
paradise, 10, 22, 23, 35, 37–42,
     83
  recognition of Manifestation
       is, 38–39
perceptions will increase dur-
     ing, 94
prayer for good-pleasure of God
     at time of death, 125–27
prayers for the departed,
     121–24, 127–30
preparation for, in this world,
     80–85
recognition of others in, 12,
     94–96
reward and punishment in, 11,
     22, 27–29, 33, 52, 82–85
  chastisement, 125
  destiny of true believer, 10,
       12–13, 21, 27–28, 41–42
  infidels, 13
should look forward to, 87
spiritual mysteries will be solved
     in, 94–95
timelessness of, 87
true life is life of spirit, 3
work done by souls during, 87

Maids of Heaven, 10
Man, 4–5. *See also* Death, physical;
     Death, spiritual; Deeds;
     Life, physical; Life, spiritu-
     al; Life after death; Soul
  ambition of, is heavenly civiliza-
       tion, 59
  body of, 34

Man *(continued)*
   confined to physical world,
     74–75
   disintegration of, 55
   respect for, 34
   soul's relation to, 7, 13–15,
     54–59, 61–69, 74–76
   creation of. *See* Creation
   discoveries and inventions of, 8,
     10, 69–73, 78
   the arts, 8, 10
   education and development of,
     86–87
   evolution of, 79–80, 86
   fate and predestination of,
     19–20
   lower nature of, 85
   mind of, 60–62, 64–67, 76
     intermediary between soul
      and body, 60–61
     rational faculty, 18–19
     reality of man is thought, 64
     true and imaginary thoughts,
      70–73
   mirror of God, 4
   station of
     crowning-point of creation,
      57
     superior to all other created
      beings, 64
Manifestations of God
   appearance of, is Day of Resur-
     rection, 35–36
   belief of, in other worlds of
     God, 12
   intercession of, 93
   lay down lives as ransom, 103
   like unveiled flower, 26
   purpose of, 10–12
   recognition of, is paradise, 38,
     39
   visions of, 71–73
Materialism, 59. *See also* World,
     transitory worthlessness of
Mediums, 98
Mind. *See* Man, mind of
Moses, 35, 72–73
Muḥammad, 36

Paradise. *See* Life after death
Parents
   children's duties toward, 92
   prayer for forgiveness of, 127
Peter, Saint, 89
Prayers
   for acceptance of fate, 20
   for the departed, 121–30
     importance of, 97–98, 104
     obligatory Prayer for the
      Dead, 121
   for forgiveness, 127–29
     of parents, 127
   for good-pleasure of God at
     time of death, 125–27
   for intercession and mercy of
     God, 124–25
Predestination, 19–20
Prophets. *See* Manifestations of
     God
Psychic phenomena. *See* Dreams;
     Extrasensory perception

Qur'án, quotation from, 84

Rational faculty. *See* Man, mind of
Reality, 24
Recognition of others in next
     world, 12, 94–96
Reincarnation, 105–07
Remoteness from God, 23
Resurrection, 23, 35–36, 38

Satan, 85–86
Sins
   forgiveness of, 129
   wash away, 127, 128
Sleep, 7, 66, 69. *See also* Dreams
Soul, 6–11. *See also* Dreams; Life,
     spiritual; Life after death
   body and, relation of, 7, 13–15,
     54–59, 61–69, 74–76
     body without a soul dies, 65
     physical frame is throne of in-
      ner temple, 34
   of children, 99–101
   development and progress of,
     6–8, 57–59, 79–82, 85–91

through acts of others, 91
attaining presence of God,
    9–10, 21, 88
through bounty of Lord, 91
through charity, 80, 92
education through opposites,
    86–87
grades and stations of souls,
    12, 95–96
through intercession, 91–93
steps to achieving perfections,
    80–81
discoveries made after death by,
    94–95
discoveries of, made through
    power of spirit, 8, 10,
    69–73, 78
immortality of, 9, 21, 55
of lower creatures, 53
mind and, relation of, 60–62,
    64–67
nature of, 8–9, 53
    after death, can never be de-
        scribed, 10
    Holy Spirit works through
        soul, 53
    is a mystery, 7–8
    is indestructible, 45, 68
    is phenomenal yet eternal,
        55–56
    mirror, 54–55, 56, 61
    suffering felt by soul, 63
proof of existence of, 45–50,
    68–69
ranks of different souls, 95–96
state of soul after death depends

on God's pleasure, 126
of true believer, 22
power of faithful soul, 9
Spirituality. See Life, spiritual
Spouse, death of, 102–03
Suicide, 102

Time, 87
Titanic disaster, 103–105

Universe, 56. See also Creation;
    Worlds of God

Visions, 71–73
Volition, 5

Wealth, true, 37
Will, free, 5
World. See also Creation
    movement necessary to exist-
        ence, 88–91, 108–09
    transitory worthlessness of,
        24–29; 108–11, 116, 117
        black in eye of dead ant, 25
        dust-heap, 118
        storehouse of affliction, 102
        vapor in desert, 24, 110
Worlds of God, 11, 16–17; See also
    Dreams
    holy and spiritually glorious, 3
    infinite, 103
    invisible realms, 52
    soul is harbinger of, 7–8

Youth. See Children